DEDICATION

This book is dedicated to all

those who believe or think,

'There has to be another way'.

Published by Purgl Publishing, The Paddock, Newburgh, Fife, KY14 6AD
Scotland UK

ISBN: 9780955262531

DISCLAIMER:

This publication contains the experience, opinion and ideas of its author. It is sold with the understanding that the author and publisher are not engaged in rendering health services in the book. The reader should consult his or her own medical and health providers as appropriate before adopting any of the suggestions in this book or drawing inferences from it. The author and publisher specifically disclaim all responsibility for any liability, loss, or risk, personal or otherwise, which is incurred as a consequence, directly or indirectly, of the use and application of any of the contents of this book.

ACKNOWLEDGMENTS

My biggest source of professional learning has come from the interactions I have had with patients. Thank you to everyone who has received my services whether that was when I was in the Health Service, or since I became fully self-employed. You always show me where the limits of my knowledge lie and therefore the areas in which I need to improve. This stimulates my ongoing learning.

Robert, thank you for giving me the title to this book all those years ago and for our continuing contact.

I have always been a great fan of cartoons. My inability to draw leads me to so admire cartoonists who can make a single line so incredibly expressive. Loz (known to me as Lawrence), who was Young Cartoonist of the year in 2012 drew the cartoon on the cover of this book. It delights me every time I look at it. Thank you so much Lawrence. He can be contacted via www.loz-art-productions.com.

Jean Jarvis, Mike Shilson, and Jeff Imrie, each read chunks of the manuscript and suggested improvements. Thank you for taking the time and trouble and I hope that most of your suggestions have been incorporated in this book. I value our friendship deeply.

Bestselling author Mary Turner Thomson (The Bigamist; The Psychopath) has been my advisor and guide through the mechanics of all aspects of book production. You have led me by the hand through the whole process Mary, I am very grateful to you for your expertise, experience, knowledge and approachability. I couldn't have done it without you.

Liz Oliver, my partner, filleted this book down to more manageable size and readability. (I have to accept that a number of my innovations and single patent have been erased. Ouch!)

Thank you for putting up with my firks and quoibles with such grace and humour, as well as sharing our lives in a similar and beautiful way.

Doctor Harry Ramnarine in Trinidad and I have shared knowledge, thoughts, discussions, suggestions about our work since 1989. He is the most innovative Doctor I know. It is a joy for me to know Harry and his family. Our contact continues. You have taught me so much Harry, thank you.

I'm very grateful to Hermen Grondijs in Holland for introducing me to new techniques to improve diagnostics and healing and for sharing both friendship and expertise.

Patricia Ramaer made taking the mugshot a pleasure rather than a pain. Thank you Patricia for your ease and professionalism.

My field of fascination regarding frequencies has expanded markedly since having Cyril Smith Ph.D, author of 'Electromagnetic Man,' as a thinking partner and collaborator, especially over the last 4 years.

My personal growth has accelerated over the last two decades largely because of the wisdom and knowledge of Derek O'Neill, who kindly wrote the Foreword. Derek continues to support thousands of lives around the world. Thank you Derek for all the work that you do.

CONTENTS

FOREWORD

By Derek O'Neill

Everywhere you turn at the moment, health concerns are headline news. It seems that everyone has an opinion and, of course, a vested interest. The huge issue, as I see it, is not that we are in the middle of a global pandemic, but that we are totally confused with conflicting information and don't know who to trust. Never before has it been so hard, yet so important to be able to discern the Truth.

Truth with a capital 'T' is universal and unchanging, not a subjective truth (however convincing it may seem) that comes from a narrow view. Having access to medical opinion that is delivered with Truth and with integrity is a precious commodity. Roger Melhuish is one of the rare few who you can rely on to deliver on both counts.

I've known Roger for nearly 20 years, and it was on one of our first meetings in Scotland that I went along to his clinic to see what his work was all about. After extensive testing, he told me I'd had a major shock in my childhood and that shock was still having an impact on my energy flow. I'm sure he even told me exactly at what age, but I've forgotten that bit. That certainly wasn't what I was expecting from a medical consultation! I have trained as a psycho-therapist, but this was news to me at the time. Nothing came to mind immediately so I sat with it for a few days. Sure enough, a memory popped up from my subconscious mind, about being attacked by a swarm of wasps. For sure it was traumatic, and I'd suppressed it for about three decades. Roger gave me a catalyst to unlock it, and to work on my own healing which is hugely important when I spend my life helping others.

What's impressive about all of this is that the body has all the answers. Unfortunately, because of a myriad of self-defence mechanisms and distractions, we don't know how to get those answers so we have largely sold out to 'experts', who we've put on a pedestal. These experts are trained to think along the straight lines laid down in their 'head-ucation', which inevitably provides a limited perspective.

What I really admire about Roger's work is that he has broadened his perspective way beyond his conventional medical training, to include a vast range of complementary approaches. He practises the medicine of the future by combining new technology with ancient wisdom. It is holistic in the truest sense of the word. Roger has learned to fully trust his Intuition, and tap into it in a creative and imaginative way. He is never afraid to try new things if it 'feels' right. He has a compelling drive to continually learn and improve. His technique has developed over 35 years yet continues to evolve.

What also drives him is great curiosity, not medical dogma. He focuses solely on how to serve his clients more effectively. His pioneering approach leads him to identify all the causes that are contributing to unwellness, illness and disease. He has an impressive range of techniques to treat these, while informing the client of their part in the process, so partnering them in their quest for healing and wellness.

Despite his vast experience, he also has the humility to tell every patient 'I can offer no guarantees and I can always be wrong'. He also reminds people that the core of healing is self-love and that although he will do whatever he can to support people's return to health, the greatest chunk of the work has to be done *by* themselves, *for* themselves. There is great wisdom in that.

On top of his medical knowledge, he has put in just as much work to grow as a person, and get to grips with what it means to be human. He has faced his personal demons, addressed messy issues and grown in Consciousness, all of which has opened him up to extraordinary insights and sensitivity. There are very few doctors who integrate spirituality into their work and who know that true healing is multi-dimensional. As a result of being open to all dimensions, Roger now works with greater compassion, brings a calm presence, Consciousness and depth of wisdom into every consultation. He has made a massive commitment, both personally and professionally to know what he knows. It has truly been his life's work.

I never fail to be impressed by the extent of Roger's knowledge and experience, and always enjoy being around his soft energy. I hope you can get to know him, even a little, through the pages of this book, and find great benefit from the rare and precious gifts he has to offer.

This man's a feckin genius at what he does!

Derek O'Neill, an Irishman, is a spiritual teacher, author, psychotherapist and master of martial arts. He is based in Dublin. He founded the Creacon Lodge Wellness Retreat Centre in County Wexford, Ireland. In 2012 Derek was presented with the Variety International Humanitarian Award for providing food, water, shelter to children in 11 countries, as well as building schools, colleges and a University. Derek has spoken at the Parliament of World Religions and addressed the United Nations. His aim is to empower others to maximise their potential.

*'Study hard what interests you most
in the most undisciplined, irreverent
and original manner possible.'*

Richard Feynman

'The seeds of the future exist
in the present, ignored by the orthodox
but acknowledged by the wise.'

Scalar Physics Research Center

INTRODUCTION & ANECDOTES

I am continually reminded of, and staggered by, the extraordinary wisdom, knowledge and memory that is stored at the cellular level in the Human Being. The memory of mind and brain may be fallible yet it seems that every significant event is recorded in the cells, certainly in the body energy system, along with the emotional impact that each event produced on the body. This includes the type of emotion which was embedded, the tissues and systems that were affected, and the ages at which these events happened. I find all of that remarkable and fascinating. It leaves me endlessly curious. It also reveals the factors which are at the origin of almost all illness acquired in life.

Over the last 40 years I have learned techniques which enable me to tap into this body wisdom and history. In my view this has made me much more effective as a doctor than I ever was when simply following my conventional medical training. Accessing this extraordinary wisdom holds a mirror up to the client, which reveals what their Being knows. My role is to ask the right questions. My questioning protocol has developed significantly over the years and its evolution is a continuing process. By the way, these questions are not asked directly to the conscious mind; they are asked of the body energy, which can communicate clearly with both the subconscious and the higher-conscious mind. I say nothing during the process of testing for, and gathering, the vital information that the body is holding.

This information is within all of us without exception – if you know where to look. The youngest I have tested was 10 months old, the oldest 102.

What information might be hidden within you? For instance, did you know that your body can tell that the electrical earthing in a house is abnormal? And that there is damp in a house even when the house is only 6 weeks old? More on this later.

Many years ago I read a monograph entitled: 'Talking Sense', by Doctor Richard Asher. He wrote it in the late 1960s and it was published in 1972, after his death. He explained that if the Health Service didn't do more to increase health, prevent illness and provide more rehabilitation it would soon be bankrupt. He realised that the Health Service was only dealing with established illness and essentially either removing the 'offending' organ or tissue with a scalpel or suppressing symptoms with pharmaceuticals. It was doing nothing to discover the reasons why those symptoms were there. In other words, the causes of illness were neither being sought nor addressed.

The analogy he drew was of a dripping tap producing a wet floor. He said the Health Service kept drying the floor; what we need is to turn off the tap.

Treating illness solely with drugs may suppress symptoms yet does nothing to turn off the tap. As the tap keeps dripping, the floor keeps getting wetter to the point where the current pharmaceuticals can no longer be effective, so the dose is increased.

The increased dose keeps pace with drying the floor for a short time to fail, inevitably, after a while. Then the dose is increased further: the pattern repeats.

What to do now? Of course, we will add another drug and see what that does. The pharmaceutical mix is no longer helpful, so either the dose is increased or yet another pharmaceutical is added.

At what point does someone in the system say 'Stop!', take a good look at what is *really* happening and make a fundamental change? Wee Jeanie with Rheumatoid Arthritis wants it to go away, not for it to be suppressed. Another thing she doesn't want is multiple side-effects from the multitude of drugs.

Meantime – you guessed it – the tap continues to drip incessantly, regardless of the treatment, so the floor is getting wetter still.

So why is anyone surprised when an illness recurs?

My task is to turn off the tap.

The cartoon on the covers of this book illustrates this beautifully.

With the right knowledge and tools, I can state quite emphatically that the taps can be turned off in almost every such case.

The book is divided into three parts. If you're more interested in the medical side, you may be tempted to skip to part 2, yet you may also be curious to understand who 'The Scottish Witch Doctor' really is. The first, autobiographical part is peppered with inexplicable anecdotes, which perhaps go some way to demonstrate that I was destined to find an unconventional approach in my profession.

Part 3 is more of a reference section, comprising a synopsis of my findings by condition, alongside personal stories from a number of my clients (the names have been changed appropriately to respect confidentiality).

.oOo.

Now a few anecdotes to whet your appetite for what follows.

Robert had been coming to see me intermittently over 12 years before he and his professional partner became World Rally champions.

He sent me some signed photographs with the legend:

"To Roger Melhuish 'MY WITCH DOCTOR'. Thanks for all your continuing help and support."

I called him to congratulate and thank him. He apologised for calling me a Witch Doctor, saying that he didn't know how else to describe what I do. I told him that I was delighted.

To be called a witch doctor by a World Champion is a rare accolade. To me it has a sense of fun, joy, respect and gratitude which delights me. So now, when people ask me what kind of doctor I am, I tell them:

"A World Champion calls me a Witch Doctor."

Then they ask me: "What kind of medicine do you do."

"I think of it as the Medicine of the future," I reply.

.oOo.

"Mum, would it be possible for me to go to Roger's funeral?" asked the 16-year-old Dan as they were driving home from a family funeral.

"I'm sure it would darling. Why do you ask?"

"Because he saved my life." Said Dan.

I had first seen Dan when he was just three years old. [More on 'Dan' in the 'In Their Own Write' section.]

.oOo.

My sister lived 360 miles away. I went through my testing protocol with her one time when she came to visit. I found pre-cancer. I told her she needed a test from her GP, yet there was no immediate rush, but it should be done within 12 months.

15 months later I hadn't heard from her, so I phoned and she had the test one month after our call. The test was negative, so I thought, 'Thank goodness for that. I must have been wrong and so need to change my testing'.

One year later she had another test. That was positive. Six weeks after that she was dead, from cancer, aged 33. Her youngest child was eight months old.

Sadly it wasn't my testing that was wrong, it was the hospital.

.oOo.

The specialist surgeon showed Mrs McGregor her kidney x-rays, and said that he was convinced that the abnormal kidney was cancerous. He felt so sure that he ruled out a biopsy to investigate further.

A few weeks later, Mrs McGregor came to see me. I tested her and found no indication of cancer, despite looking from multiple perspectives. We had a conversation about my findings and her resultant uncertainty. I appreciated the gravity of the decision she needed to make, and said whatever decision she made she had to be comfortable with. I also added that nobody was entitled to criticise her for whatever decision she would make.

She chose surgery.

A subsequent pathology report found no evidence of cancer.

The surgeon apologised.

.oOo.

I had tested Ted on a trip to the Channel Islands and at the end of that consultation I slid a piece of paper across to him, which said: '? Pre-cancer of the prostate.'

He came to see me when I revisited the island 12 years later. He told me he had made a promise to himself to come and see me when I was there next.

He told me his story.

After our previous consultation he had walked out to meet his wife and said: *"Well, that was a waste of time."*

Then he went on: "*Yesterday I had the 42nd and last Radiotherapy treatment for my cancer of the prostate. I need to do three things: first I want to apologise to you; second I want to thank you and third I want to give you a hug.*"

I accepted all three.

PART ONE

THE MAN

EARLY YEARS

I was born in Bristol in 1946 and was taken to Rhodesia, now Zimbabwe, when I was 6 months old. (The Scottish part of my pseudonym emerges later in the story.) Dad was in the RAF; he was posted to Rhodesia and left the UK before I was born. In his words he was the 'lowest form of life' in the RAF yet became an expert in the maintenance of the Merlin engine on Hurricanes and Spitfires. Mum was taking me to join him. We embarked on our voyage on the SS Georgic, a troop carrier, which (according to my mum) was the most uncomfortable way to travel. Despite the promise of adventure and the reunion to look forward to at the end of the trip, it was a gruelling experience. A highlight for her was when her brother, my Uncle Vic, boarded the ship at Port Said on the Suez Canal, to meet her and me for the first time. Uncle Vic was a vehicle mechanic with C platoon of the 51st Company Royal Army Service Corps (RASC) and was given permission to have time off to leave his unit to meet his sister. He saw me before my dad did.

The ship docked in South Africa and we went by rail to Rhodesia.

Dad was living on a smallholding of a few hundred acres. Jessie, a delightful African lady who worked there, soon became known to me as 'Nanny'. She looked after me as if I was her own child. Jessie played with me, took me with her wherever she went, sang to me, laughed with me. She was my constant source of care and companionship, and consequently we were incredibly close.

My sense of this time spent with Jessie was of vitality, vibrancy and wholeheartedness. I felt wanted and included as an integral part of her life. She doted on me. I remember that I didn't wear shoes during this time, feeling so carefree as I played with the local children. To this day I love bright colours and really hot sunshine. These are the visceral reminders of this precious time when I felt truly loved and cherished.

Aside from Jessie, I have very few memories from that time. What I can recall is the taste and smell of the native bread, the white kraals with their conical thatched roofs and the vibrant colours. When I came back from Rhodesia aged four, I was bilingual in Shona and English. I pleaded with my parents to have Jessie come home with us, but to no avail; we couldn't afford it, and we had nowhere for her to stay. She was heartbroken and, on reflection, I know I was too. I never felt that level of love again. On the boat home I remember chewing the ship's rail which was white, the paint in those days being leaded. It couldn't have tasted very pleasant but I can only surmise that the mix of frustration, anger, sadness and grief was seeking an outlet. My mother was never really tactile. I don't ever remember calling her 'Mum', instead choosing a derivation of her Christian name. She never seemed to mind it, yet it speaks volumes about our relationship.

Back in the UK, we were living in a small house close to a pub in Redcliffe near Bristol. This house belonged to my great Aunt Annie. Aunt Annie was apparently a formidable woman. She was a large lady and had been matron of Guy's Hospital in London. Before moving to Redcliffe, she and her husband had lived in Arch Road, Bristol. While in Arch Road they had looked after my mother, who was sent to Annie's to stay for a while when her brother Mervyn developed typhus. Annie so enjoyed looking after mum that she became quite resolute in not letting her go back home. Annie told my mother, Winn, that Winn's own mother did not want her to go back and stay in the family home. Uncle Vic assures me this is not true. Winn was definitely wanted back, but sadly never returned. Instead, she stayed with Aunt Annie – a 'triumph' of this formidable lady's determination. For the rest of her life, my mother believed the story that she was not wanted by her own mother and was never able to let go of her anger and resentment. Very sad.

Meantime I went from feeling loved, included, cherished and seen, to being a child who was seen but not heard, sitting alone and feeling unloved. The brightness and warmth of Africa were replaced by the drab, bland greyness of our new life in the UK . It was a devastating change.

Shortly after our return from Rhodesia, my Uncle Vic and Auntie Eira took me, with some other friends and families, on a coach trip to Minehead. It turned out to be a memorable visit. At Minehead at the time was a stone-built paddling pool which filled up every time the tide came in. The stone wall enclosing it had a flat top which I could walk along and as I was doing so, something extraordinary happened. This is Uncle Vic's verbatim description of the event.

"You fell into the water. In an instant you were in the water and then back out. It was amazing. You were in and back out again as if you had walked on water. You were out in an instant, so quick I didn't even have time to move to you. It was like a film run backwards, you getting out."

They took off my wet clothes and I wore their friend Ron's jacket all the way home in the coach. To this day Uncle Vic says that was the day I walked on water. Certainly no one else was visible around me, no one gave me a push, nor a helping hand to get out. Vic saw the whole thing and is as mystified and amazed today as he was then. He is now 94.

I think that was the first time that I can remember when my guardian angels, some mysterious supporting and caring force, came to my rescue. I don't know what else to call that energy, yet I am eternally grateful to it and for it. I have trusted in the presence of that power ever since.

The only reason I know so much about my mother's background is because Uncle Vic is still alive and has given me the information. Thank you Uncle Vic!

I know much less about my father. All I know is that he was born in London. His father returned from the First World War and the only job my grandfather could get was selling matches on the street in London. He could not really afford to look after my father, so dad was sent to Derbyshire, I think to relatives who lived on a farm. At some stage he returned to London and, at age 14, he got a job in the Marconi factory sweeping the floor. At the age of 16 he joined the RAF where he met my mother.

On my fifth birthday I had been given a toy gun which fired caps. These were little dots of explosive powder imprinted on a long, narrow strip of paper that was loaded into the gun and which went 'bang' when hit by the hammer of the gun. These strips of caps were stored in small circular paper containers. I think I had three of those containers and for some reason I had taken the strips out of their containers and put them in my left trouser pocket.

Armed and ready, I headed off to a party at my friend Paul's house. Their open fire was burning, the room was warm and full of schoolfriends and I was standing at the back of the group. I recall being entranced by the Lone Ranger who was galloping across the television screen (we didn't have a TV in our house) as someone brushed past me. Suddenly I could smell burning. My pocket was on fire. The friction must have ignited the caps. Instinctively, I put my left hand in to take out the ignited caps; consequently, my hand was badly burnt and so was my thigh. I had to go to Bristol Royal Infirmary to have the burns dressed. Each finger was swathed in layers of tubular dressings and my whole hand was bandaged. It looked like a boxing glove with fingers. I remember going to play cricket somewhere and they made me wicket-keeper because I already had a glove on. There's definitely some juvenile logic in that.

Whether my hospital experience had literally ignited something within me, I'll never know but sometime between my fifth and sixth birthday I had a sudden realisation: I was going to become a doctor. This affirmation did seem to come out of the blue. There was no one remotely medical in the family, nor had anyone in the family been to university. As I have already mentioned, Dad was in the RAF, and Mum was a clerical assistant in an office nearby. All my school friends at the time wanted to be train drivers; something I had no interest in at all. No-one I knew was remotely interested in medicine.

What impresses me about that realisation is the certainty that I felt around it. To me it was an absolute truth; I was going to become a doctor. Relatives would ask me at weddings and similar gatherings:

"And what are you going to be when you grow up?"

And I would always answer, "I'm going to be a doctor."

But I could never understand why they would laugh and say, "We'll see."

My brother Peter was born two years after we got back to Bristol. Auntie Annie had died before we came back to Britain. We lived in her old house along with her widowed husband. My mother had to look after a new-born, an old man and me. Dad was posted elsewhere and would only come home for occasional weekends or periods of leave. This meant that for a lot of the time I was left to my own devices. I had discovered reading, which meant that I was out of the way and I could learn so much. I was avid for knowledge and consumed any factual text, especially encyclopaedias. This satisfied me mentally, yet emotionally I was profoundly lonely. Mum was busy with Peter who had asthma and had to go to hospital every day, and the old man was ailing more. Mum had so much on her plate. The daily visits to hospital stopped after mum had been taught percussion to treat Peter's chest, but it still took considerable time for her to administer his daily treatment at home. Then the old man became progressively more unwell and mum's availability for me was diminished even more. I was clothed well and fed, yet felt emotionally barren.

I simply felt in the way, and a sense of isolation and sadness grew. Still only six years old I started to see no point in living. Life seemed incredibly mechanical. Get up, dress, eat breakfast, go to school, come home, eat, read, go to bed. Repeat. I could see no way out. The mental turmoil, the feeling of being in the way, what I now recognise as feeling unloved, created a relentless heartache which was constantly painful. Then, one Sunday, I realised there was an answer. That is: life was too painful so I could simply stop living. The relief that realisation brought was incredible. The turmoil was replaced with clarity and a beautiful sense of peace.

Mum had made me a terry-towelling dressing gown which had a belt made of the same material. I took the belt off and went into the bathroom. There was a small window that had a long, perforated metal arm which you unhooked and pushed out to open. I unhooked the metal arm so that it was at 90° to the window frame, and protruding out into the bathroom. I tied one end of my belt to that arm and the other end around my neck. I stepped off the chair I'd been standing on and kicked it away. As I hung there an amazing thing happened. I thought:

"This is *not* the answer. There has to be another way."

Immediately, another thought came to mind, "What if I'm too late? What if I can't get out of this?"

I started to laugh at myself and my predicament. I honestly don't know how I got out of that. Did my feet contact the upturned chair? Everything as to how this happened is conjecture. Perhaps it was another time when my guardian angels intervened, but I'm very glad now I didn't succeed.

As a result of this I have great empathy for anyone who is suicidal. Curiously, I suppressed all of this for several decades until it was unlocked during a period of intensive counselling. By way of closure, there was a knot in the dressing gown belt which I wasn't able to undo until around 2003 (over 50 years after the incident), after I had explained to my mother why the knot was there. She was horrified and deeply apologetic.

I remember the old man in the house dying, but I don't remember his funeral. I have a vague notion that I may have been sent to London to avoid that event. I remember being put on the train at Bristol Temple Meads station on my own and told to get off in London. I remember that people in the carriage were very solicitous telling me when the train stopped that it wasn't yet at London. I imagine that today putting a six or seven-year-old on a train alone would be subject to parental neglect and the full force of the Law. In those days it seemed people were very much more caring of others and understanding and cooperative in attitude. Folk were much more trusting, much less paranoid. Perhaps that is one legacy of the post-war period.

From as early as I can recall, I have always been very imaginative and creative – not in an artistic sense but in the formation of ideas. Still in my early years at primary school, I remember watching dad using a screwdriver. I said to him if there was more than one groove in the top of the screw and an equivalent change in the screwdriver there would be more purchase on the screw and it will be easier to drive it home. With a slightly bemused expression, he told me that the Phillips screwdriver already existed.

Also around age 5 or 6, I was reading about big ships and how they rolled and pitched in bad weather. So I came up with the idea of stubby wings sticking out from the hull under the water to damp down the rolling, and of a bulbous protrusion at the bow, again underwater, to reduce pitching. That led me to think about ways of reducing drag in a boat and I came up with the idea of wings which lifted the hull from the water, nowadays called hydrofoils.

When my parents bought a radio, they switched it on and then instructed me to look at it when it was playing. I was immediately able to reason that this didn't make any sense. The radio was just sitting there and my ability to hear it did not depend on the way I was facing.

They were out one time so I unplugged the radio and took it apart to see what was in it. What struck me was that the valves were connected by lengths of insulated wire which snaked across the chassis of the radio. These wires had to be cut, have insulation removed at each end, placed along their serpentine path and connected to the relevant components. This all had to be done by hand. I couldn't understand why the wires were not pre-built into the chassis under-surface so that all the operatives had to do was to insert the valves.

A year or so before that my father was taking apart the dynamo from a car (alternators were yet to come). I was fascinated, especially by the shiny copper wiring making the bulk of the rotor. I asked him what it did and how it worked. He told me. I looked at it and said to him, "You know, if you made that copper piece flat and made the enclosure flat as well and put current in each then the magnetism would have the one floating above the other, and the floating one might move."

Dad looked at it for the longest time and then said, "You might well be right."

Now trains are running on maglev. The first commercial passenger use of maglev was not until 1984.

I have no idea where these remarkable insights came from. Over the years, I have had so many more innovative ideas than I've had the time, energy or inclination to do anything with. In fact, one patent I was granted came to nothing, despite a significant outlay of time and money. Perhaps again my guardian angels have been working hard to keep me on the right track, putting a stop to the many distractions that have continued to arise with intriguing regularity.

SCHOOL DAYS

My first school was Barnard's Place Infants School in Redcliffe, Bristol. The first of a sparse selection of memories from that time is the daily habit of everyone having a lie down on camp beds for the first half-hour after lunch. We all had an emblem for the bed allocated, mine was a fish. Another ritual was chanting the times tables. The fortunate side-effect of this practice was that if you didn't know an answer, the majority of the rest of the class provided it and so these tables became embedded in memory.

Another distinctly less palatable memory is of being served boiled fish one lunchtime. Ah, the wonders of 1950's school dinners! I remember the fish as being a white mush with bones sticking out of it and covered by a red sauce which tasted ghastly and whose relationship to tomato was at best approximate. We had to show our plate to the teacher after the meal to show that we had eaten everything. I felt dreadful after the first mouthful, showed the plate to the teacher who told me to go and eat some more. I went back to my place, put my plate down and walked back home. I felt terrible. I remember walking past a lady who was coming the other way and she asked me if I was all right. Whether I answered her or not I don't recall but when I got home, I knocked on the door, Mum opened it, and was both surprised and alarmed to see me. She said I looked green. To this day I have no stomach for boiled fish.

My next school was Windmill Hill Primary School. One day the class was given a whole load of new books. I was asked to unpack them and lay them out on the table. I held onto the encyclopaedia, whilst everyone else was invited to come to the table and choose a book. Then the teacher asked everyone what they had chosen and praised them for their choice of novel. When it came to my turn he said: "But that's an encyclopaedia!" as if it was somehow wrong to choose something that gave me more knowledge.

At the age of eight we moved to Little Stoke, north of Bristol, and I was moved to another primary school. There were acres of fields across the road, with a pond in the corner opposite the house, and school was an easy walk every day. There were two lots of woods within reach, one was called Savage's Wood which was furthest away. For any curious boy, they were great places to walk to, explore and play in.

At the age of 14 I got a Saturday job in the local butcher's shop. It was my job to thoroughly clean the big walk-in fridge and the wooden racks within it. I delivered orders on my butcher's bike. I really enjoyed the job and Ray, the master butcher, was a good teacher and boss. It taught me to recognise the link between work and money. It also taught me how to sharpen a knife on a steel, how to recognise the different meats, how to gut poultry (doing some 20 chickens a day in the run-up to Christmas), how to clean anything no matter how clarty (dirty) it might be, and how to get on with people.

For a time, I also had a paper round along with the job at the butchers, yet when I found that the paper round interfered with the Saturday job, I gave up delivering newspapers.

The job at the butchers had another unexpected benefit to my education. Now at Thornbury Grammar School, in one biology lesson we were told we were going to have to dissect an eyeball. I offered to supply some and early in the morning of that lesson I went to the butchers, cut the eyes out of several cows' heads and took them to school.

Although you may think that this was leading me nicely into a career in surgery, my forte was languages, especially French. I was told by my teacher that I was useless at Maths, so that's exactly what I believed and consequently achieved very little. Similarly in Art, I took a drawing to the teacher and asked how I could improve it. Rather than offer any constructive advice, he merely commented that I could not draw. So, again, that's exactly what I achieved. In fact, I never did another moment of art in those double periods. I took a book in with me and read throughout that time. The teacher was entirely unperturbed by my disinterest in his subject, and never commented on my abject refusal to produce anything. I've since learned that drawing can be taught. Pioneering physicist Richard Feynman is one of my heroes. He learned to draw in his 40s to the point of having exhibitions under a different name. Andrew Matthews, the author of 'Being Happy', was also taught to draw. So, I now believe that the mechanics of art can be taught. That said, I describe myself as having the mathematical and artistic equivalent of dyslexia. Despite being very visual when I am thinking creatively, I struggle to translate that in to images on paper.

When we were approaching O-level exams I asked the Careers master what careers my current studying would make available to me. He told me I could be a Librarian! When asked what would enable me to get to medical school, he said I would have to do A-level sciences, specifically Physics, Chemistry, and Biology. Because of my facility with French, they agreed to adjust the whole curriculum so that I could do these four A-levels.

Mr Hodge, the assistant headmaster, who had rearranged the whole sixth form curriculum just for me, was mortified when I told him that Dad was moving to Coventry and I would be leaving after the O-levels. I had really enjoyed Thornbury Grammar School and had wanted to stay there but Dad, rightly, insisted we all go together to Coventry.

Following the move, Dad worked with Rolls-Royce Aero engines. I went to King Henry VIII School. This was an all boys school, whereas before I was used to a co-educational environment.

At secondary school, I embarked on what would be a fairly short but enjoyable relationship with sport. I was in the school gymnastics team and got a place in the Rugby 3rds. It was all quite light and fun; the problem for me was that it interfered with my Saturday job.

By the age of 16, I was the eldest of 5 siblings and we had recently moved to Coventry. I was eager to find weekend work to replace my butcher's job. I responded to an advert in the evening paper for an assistant wanted at the Carpet Store in Coventry market on Saturdays. Enticed by the prospect of something a bit different and a welcome source of income, I went to see Maurice Cohn, who owned the Birmingham-based outfit. He interviewed me and offered me the job.

We had a display on the outside of the market, carpets and rugs draped everywhere, while on the inside there was a stall for the more expensive rugs. I was nominated to help with the inside stall alongside Brian. When those who had bought a carpet needed it fitted in their home it was Brian who did that work, but on Saturdays he always supervised the inside stall. He was a great teacher, principally about life itself and about sex in particular. This was music to the ears of a tumescent teenager. Sales only took part of our time, the rest of our time was spent watching the people go by, especially the younger ladies.

It was a wonderful education.

I also learned a lot about how to talk with people, how to listen and how to adjust my approach and language depending on whom I was speaking with.

At some point, a student teacher called Tony joined us at the Carpet Store. His girlfriend lived in a flat with four other female student teachers. Tony, doing his bit for his new mate, introduced me to one of them – a beautiful girl called Maggie who became my first proper girlfriend. I was 17 at the time. She was tall, slim, had long blonde hair, was intelligent, sensitive and delightful company. She seemed to have a truly etheric beauty that I have never forgotten. I spent as much time with her as I could. One time I went round to her flat all I could smell was baby talcum powder. Apparently, it was the one night in the week when they turned the boiler on full so that they could each have a bath; the baby talc was an integral part of the bathing ritual.

A great joy for me was taking Maggie for a drive in Betsy, my jalopy, especially on a Sunday. To this day my heart sings when I see a carpet of bluebells, it always reminds me of Maggie. That relationship had a purity and beauty about it which is hard to express, although there was no carnal aspect to it at all. One of her flat mates had introduced me to sex, which I found completely underwhelming at the time. I couldn't understand what the fuss was all about. Now that I have experienced the true beauty of love-making I'm extremely grateful for that disappointing first experience – I don't think I'd have finished University otherwise!

At 17 years of age, aside from Maggie, my only other love was cars.

I digress – at this point in the first draft of my writing this chapter, I jumped straight in to stories of my amateur mechanics. I waxed lyrical about my beloved early cars and my time with Dad spent tinkering away on engines for hours in our garage. But alas, my editor deemed it unsuitable for a book primarily on medicine so it was digitally shelved. But I must mention the best car I ever had and which is still sitting in my garage awaiting some tender, loving care: a Rousesport 304R. Andy Rouse, doyen of Saloon Car racing, modified the Ford Cosworth. It has Ferrari performance, 4-wheel drive, 5 seats, a big boot and Ford running costs. It is a brilliant car yet has not been on the road for 15 years. What a waste!

As I've mentioned earlier, I seemed to acquire a kind of mechanical intuition. I really enjoyed learning how things work, how they interact and interrelate. Spending time doing something so constructive, which had a tangible and enjoyable outcome, filled me with fascination and fulfilment. The time spent with Dad, witnessing his knowledge and creativity, always finding the solution to a problem because he did not have all the necessary tools, was inspiring and bonding. It must have been from him that I learned that no matter what the problem there is always a solution, all we have to do is find it. Hopefully I have passed this philosophy on to my children as well.

I had no idea at the time that my endless curiosity would eventually enable me to jalouse the subtle, magical links between cause and effect in the suffering human being. I love working that out. That fascination has no limits. Now I think I am the richest man in the world in terms of fulfilment. I love it.

Does this vital part of my work have its origins in my re-fettling cars? It may well do.

Perhaps the best example of my mechanical intuition was at Silverstone,a motor racing circuit, in 1967. I was in the Pits at Silverstone on the Saturday of practising for the

British Grand Prix the next day, just watching the action, when I saw the Lotus 49 for the first time. It had the new Cosworth engine, which to me was a mechanical sculpture. Yet there was something about the car which didn't quite fit. Then I just 'saw' what it was. The car was the wrong shape. It needed to be more wedge-shaped, with the radiators either side of the driver. Other specifics were clear in my vision too – the underside had to be an inverted aerofoil section, so generating more downforce the faster it went. The brakes would be inboard, so reducing the unsprung mass of the wheels, yet they would need to be ventilated.

I was a few steps away from Colin Chapman, the design genius behind Lotus, and was about to take the few steps towards him to offer my ideas. I stopped myself. Who was I to tell the premier race-car designer in the world that his car was the wrong shape? As a medical student, I had zero credibility in any engineering field. I sat down again and continued my musings, deciding it prudent to keep my opinions to myself. Interestingly, in 1970 the Lotus 72 was launched which incorporated all that I had 'seen'. It is still the design that has won more Grand Prix than any other. My vision was vindicated.

BEING A MEDICAL STUDENT

In my final year at King Henry VIII school, despite my total lack of natural flair for traditional sciences, I scraped through with the necessary grades to go to medical school. After a bit of research, helpfully guided by our family doctor who was Scottish, I opted for St Andrews.

St Andrews is the perfect place for a university. A small town with a ruined cathedral and castle, the University is the oldest in Scotland having been founded in 1413, plus its fabled golf courses. It is a place of gentle dignity, grey stone houses and expansive beaches. Everywhere is in walking distance. It is a beautiful and idyllic environment in which to grow and learn. Little did I know just how much I'd fall in love with the place and come to make Scotland my adopted home. (I'm still here 55 years later and, marvelling at the majestic view over the Forth of Tay that I savour every day, I just can't imagine wanting to live anywhere else.)

Including postgraduates, the University numbered some 1500 souls when I started and so I was on nodding acquaintance with many of them. Additionally, the University has a tradition where every first-year student, called a Bejant (from the French *bec jaune*, fledgling) has a third year student or above as a Senior Man and a Senior Woman to help integrate the new student into the ways of university life. It is a great system.

Culture and history seem to be embedded everywhere in St Andrews. One of the many traditions is the annual 'Raisin Monday'. It sounds innocent enough: in return for the help provided by the Senior Man and Senior Woman, the Bejant, traditionally, would give a pound of raisins to each of these academic parents. Since raisins are dried grapes, and a popular liquid is made from fermented crushed grapes, raisins no longer seem to be accepted currency. Wine, indeed any form of alcohol in a bottle, is a very acceptable alternative. In return for this liquid gift, the Bejant receives a raisin receipt. This receipt is written in Latin and any third-year student or above can demand to see the receipt. If they think there is a flaw in the Latin, (and their word is final on this matter) the Bejant has to sing aloud a verse of Gaudeamus Igitur there and then to whomever is assembled. My raisin receipt was a suitably inscribed plastic potty, with the University shield painted in the base. My potty got a lot of scrutiny.

Raisin receipts can be roughly categorised into those that are portable and those that you need to stay with. Huge imagination goes to their creation. Seeing a Bejant walking around wearing one scuba flipper bearing a Latin inscription; another dragging a ball and chain, yet another inside a temporary stockade. All the Bejants eventually reach the Quad. The whole atmosphere is of fun and slapstick. Everyone lets their hair down.

Raisin Monday seems to be a tradition which really welcomes the Bejants into the academic family, which is actually the whole student body.

First year medical students at St Andrews had to undergo what I guess would be a form of induction, a rite of passage, called the Bejant Hecklings. This happened early in the first term – the 2nd and 3rd year medics were sworn to secrecy regarding what form their induction took. In the spirit of this tradition, I'll keep the details of my own experience to myself but, safe to say, it was distinctly more bearable than I had imagined.

A curious and subtle change happened after these Hecklings: I really felt part of the medical student body, almost as if it was a family. When I spoke to the 2nd and 3rd year medics, they all said they had similar feelings.

Unlike Raisin Monday, which still goes on, it seems that these Hecklings are no longer part of the medical student experience at St Andrews. I don't know why that is because I found it to be fun and bonding and would suggest that it might be resumed.

In those days our class numbered 40 people, so everyone knew everybody and great friendships developed. The medical course was intense; the only time we were not in a lecture theatre or laboratory was a Wednesday afternoon. That was the time allocated for sport. On my first Wednesday afternoon I went along to the sports hall looking to do gymnastics. Evidently, there was no gymnastics club so that enquiry was my only dip into sports while I was at university.

Mental decompression and socialising revolved around the pub or a pier walk, a stroll along the West Sands or one of the academic parents might be having a sherry party on a Saturday afternoon. It was just another excuse for a party. Most faculties had an annual ball, and the Bute Medical Society Ball was traditionally the first of the season. One year, as convener of the ball, I was obliged to stay until the invited academic guests had left. My best friend from school was getting married the next day in Leeds. So, I drove down to Leeds overnight and, having had no sleep, delivered the worst best man's speech you've ever heard. Sorry Roger and Chris!

Another decompression was to go to 'The Himalayas', a hilly putting green between the Old Course and the West

Sands. The nonsense of trying to get this tiny ball to negotiate the contours and drop into the cup provided a consuming and welcome diversion.

Charities Week was always great fun. On one occasion I went into a local butcher's shop and bought some hot pies, which we intended to auction off to the students during a class to raise money for charity. My partner in crime was an Arts student, coincidently, also called Maggie. We selected the main auditorium in the Arts building as our target. The plan was that she would go into the back of the lecture hall, join the lecture and would indicate to me whether to go ahead or not. But our plan had a flaw – I had to be inside the lecture hall before I could actually see Maggie to tell whether it would be 'go' or 'no-go'. Anyway, I went in; the lecture was in full swing. I jovially apologised to the lecturer for the intrusion and said I was there to auction pies to his hungry students. There was a stunned silence. I looked into the auditorium to find Maggie making herself as small as possible at the back of the lecture theatre shaking her head, whilst desperately trying to stop herself laughing out loud at my discomfort. It turned out that I had interrupted a visiting Professor from Oxford who was giving an annual invitational lecture – a very special and prestigious event! The Professor who had invited him said that he didn't think this was quite the moment for me to go ahead with my plan. It was one of those horrible, heart-sinking 'uh-oh' moments. I apologised to both the professors, in a somewhat more sombre tone, and me and the pies made a hasty retreat.

Later in the day I went back to find the local Prof to apologise. I was suitably relieved to find that he was quite delightful and thanked me for seeing him. He said that both he and his colleague from Oxford had come out after the lecture to look for me and buy some pies! But by that time, I had skedaddled, wreathed in embarrassment.

Another year, I had an inspired idea to 'kidnap' the pop group The Kinks. They had a gig at the Raith Ballroom in Kirkcaldy. We contacted their manager who, having been reassured that we were not *actually* planning to kidnap the guys, said we could come along and get our photograph taken with the group. Alison, the Charities Queen, the Charities Convener and myself drove off to Kirkcaldy on our mission. The guys took it in great spirit, we got our photo and as a bonus got to listen to their concert free of charge!

Clearly, the point of the stunt was to generate publicity for our Charities Week so I phoned most of the daily papers later that evening; after all we had a photo to prove we had 'got them'. None were interested. The typical reply from the Night Editor was, "Who or what on earth are the Kinks?"

They weren't that famous at that time, yet Ray Davies' songs have since become classics.

Disappointingly, while it was a good laugh and a great experience, it had zero impact in generating any additional money.

On another occasion we went to Glasgow to rattle our collecting tins at a Rangers versus Celtic football match. We had the legal permits to do this but were still reliant on the police who took us in to watch the match. I remember thinking I'd never seen policemen who were quite so big and realised how intimidating a large police horse can be when standing right next to you. The Celtic fans were on our left and the Rangers fans to our right. Thankfully our bright red gowns elicited no tribal conflict from either group, yet it was still deemed necessary to position us within the substantial gap between the rival fans. I don't remember the score, just the noise, the great Glaswegian banter and their generosity.

The final Saturday of Charities Week always saw a parade through the town of floats created by each hall of residence and some of the clubs at the University. The creativity was amazing. The lorries were provided by a local transport company and we had free reign on how they were transformed. Our Hall of residence, St Regulus Hall, always known as 'Regs', made the lorry look like a ship converted to a pirate radio station. I remember lying on a platform about a foot off the ground with tinfoil from the waist down, dressed as a mermaid. Walking alongside me to ensure that I stayed safe was a classmate who went on to become a Consultant Orthopaedic Surgeon in Manchester. Children in the crowd would point to me and say, "Ooo look Daddy, a mermaid!"

Anything for charity!

I accepted an invitation to become the Charities Convener for the following year. After a few months I realised it would take far too much of my time and, sadly, had to resign the post.

One role I did fulfil was as President of the Bute Medical Society, as I had been voted in by my classmates. My inaugural address to the medical students was about car design and road accident injury. It was one of the few chances I got to allow my interest in cars and medicine to overlap.

As President, I was lucky enough to represent the medical students of St Andrews at other medical societies' special occasions, ranging from the 150th anniversary of the Edinburgh University Medical Society to a UK wide medical student invitation to go to Belfast for a long weekend conference. My Vice President was Sheena. We took the ferry across to Belfast and poor Sheena was seasick (something that, thankfully, I have never experienced).

On our first evening I left Sheena to rest and recover while I was invited out by one of my host students. He took me to a bar in Belfast and asked me what I would like to drink. In Ireland, there really was no choice was there? I asked the barman for a pint of Guinness. He looked at me realising that I was a stranger and said:

"Would you like Double X, Treble X or Porter?"

Being a novice, I asked what the difference was. He replied:

"Double X is very good, Treble X is very, very good and Porter is excellent."

I chose the Porter. It seemed to fall out of the tap in just 2 or 3 lumps. It tasted velvety and delicious. What surprised me was that my host student asked for a hot toddy. The barman didn't bat an eyelid and served him his drink. I didn't realise that hot toddies were available in any bar.

Sheena joined me the next morning at breakfast. She had recovered well and was great company. One evening there was a competition for all the delegates. I remember it included playing darts, bottle walking and limbo dancing plus other games. We won! I did the lowest limbo and farthest bottle walk and did well at darts too. I can't recall the other events we competed in, but it was all informal and great fun.

On the academic front, I have a confession to make. I was a terrible student. My lack of ability in science, my mathematical dyslexia, (technically called dyscalculia) and my tendency towards more lateral thinking, was not the ideal combination. The first year in St Andrews was spent studying Physics (which at that time was called Natural Philosophy), Chemistry, Zoology and Botany. At the end of that year we had degree exams in each of these subjects. When these had finished Mike, a great buddy throughout University, and I went to the beach at Crail. We were able to identify everything we saw on the beach, all the shells all the seaweeds. We felt like David Attenborough! 10% of the class didn't pass those exams. That was the last we saw of them. Fortunately, I only had to re-sit Physics, so scraped though to the next year.

The long summer holiday meant it was time to go back to the building site, where I'd spent some time working between school and uni. It was a great way to earn some money to help pay my way through university. If it hadn't been for student grants I wouldn't have been able to do Medicine. It seems wrong that students are burdened with debt when they leave university today.

The second and third year in St Andrews was devoted to the study of Anatomy, Physiology and Biochemistry. What seemed crazy to me was that the course was not integrated. We might be studying the Anatomy of the abdomen, the Biochemistry of bones and muscles and the Physiology of respiration at the same time. Surely it made sense to look at the various aspects of each organ or system simultaneously so that the inter-connectedness of the related disciplines was apparent. Looking for an outlet for my frustrations, I asked if I could see Professor Walmsley, the Dean of the Faculty and head of the Department of Anatomy. I told him of my concerns. He replied, "Change by evolution, not revolution Mr Melhuish."

Incidentally, I was visiting the new Medical Building shortly after it had opened in 2010 when I told this story to Professor Hugh McDougall, the Dean at the time, who said, "Well Roger, it's only taken 40 years."

From my student perspective at that time, I had some concerns. Firstly, the Anatomy was taught exceptionally well yet I couldn't see the point of learning this detail at this time in our career because I wasn't going to be a surgeon tomorrow. Disuse atrophy is a phrase in medicine which is self-explanatory: if something isn't used regularly it diminishes in size and capability. An everyday example is muscles, when they are not used over a long time they diminish in bulk and strength. The same happens in learning, what you don't keep applying you forget. Why did we have to learn in this detail just to be able to pass an exam? As soon as the exam was finished that box would be closed and we would move on to another subject completely.

Secondly, I became aware of a feature of my brain at a certain time of day. Exams were run from 9 to 12 and then from 2 until 4 or 5pm. Some part of my brain always switched off between 1:15 and 2:30pm. It was the part necessary for recall. Being halfway through the alphabet, I was always scheduled at 2pm for oral exams. Even though I knew that I *knew* the answer to the question, could I locate and retrieve that answer? No. It was mortifying. The automatic retriever was asleep. To this day I don't schedule appointments in the afternoon until 2:30pm. The other component to this body clock foible is food intolerance, of which I was totally unaware throughout my student and early professional life. I didn't even know such a thing as food intolerance existed until I learned other aspects of Medicine many years later. My post-prandial malaise was due to an inability to properly digest milk products and wheat. That is still the case.

Second MB (Bachelor of Medicine) was the big hurdle exam that we *had* to pass to progress further, which was at the end of the Spring term in third year. At the start of the following summer term, Professor Sir Ian Hill addressed us and welcomed us to Dundee to begin our Clinical training. One thing he said still stands out in my mind, *"Ladies and Gentlemen, I have a confession to make. Fifty percent, of what we teach you will be wrong; I only wish I knew which fifty percent."*

This man was Dean of the Faculty of Medicine, President of the Royal College of Physicians in Edinburgh and Queen's physician in Scotland. This luminary in the field of medicine, this eminence was honest and humble. He enthused me. It was exactly what I needed to hear. This gave me the foundation to question everything I was taught rather than take it verbatim; something I continue to do.

Psychology and Statistics were taught in Dundee in the summer term. I confess that on a summer's day with the sun shining and friends from other faculties having finished their finals, playing cricket with them on the West Sands was much more fun and had vastly more attraction than these subjects in Dundee. I also remember seeing a mathematician and theoretical physicist sitting on the white line in the middle of South Street, close to the West Port, playing chess in the sunshine after their finals. That term was beautiful. It was an extremely welcome decompression after the rigours of the second MB.

Again the building site beckoned during the long summer holiday.

Fourth year was the beginning of the clinical phase of our learning. Six of us shared a house a few miles to the west of Dundee. It was owned by a poultry farmer who lived next door. His house had a swimming pool and sauna attached, which he said we could use. He would occasionally come across with a tray of eggs, or pheasant or goose for cooking. It was an idyllic place for students. Peaceful and quiet, apart from the railway line and station immediately adjacent to the house, and a great place to retreat to. We became famous for the parties we hosted there.

I spent two years in this house. In the second of those years I did a locum on the Gynaecology ward, which was notable for two things. The first was that I cheekily said to the most attractive nurse on the ward, "When are you going to take me out for a drink?"

Later in the week I was working in the ward when I got a tap on the shoulder. I turned to see this nurse who said, "Were you serious about that drink?"

Immediately I replied, "Of course I was."

"Okay. Would you be free this evening?" she said.

"Yes, but I don't know where we would go that is within walking distance." The local pubs did not look at all salubrious.

"That's okay I've got a car. We'll go to Graystane Hotel."

So after work she took me to the lounge bar. When I asked her what she would like to drink she replied, "A brandy and ginger please." I should add that this was well before drink driving became illegal.

"Look, I said, I'm a student. You have a choice. Would you like beer or lager?"

We married two years later, just five months after I graduated.

The second notable event of my time on the gynae ward was on a Sunday. I had the most embarrassing moment of my professional life.

On Sundays, patients listed for surgery on the Monday would come in to be clerked and prepared for surgery the next day. This involved a full physical examination from head to toe, taking bloods and the signing of consent forms. To cut a long story short I was completing my assessment by conducting an internal examination on one of these ladies. I was simply doing my clinical duties, prodding around down there when she let out an unfettered, "Ohoooo!!! I'm sorry … I'm sorry …" She'd had an orgasm.

I turned to see my chaperone bent over like a paperclip, clutching the sides of her chest which was heaving with suppressed laughter.

Something must have been said in the nurses' coffee lounge because after that I was conscious of curious, intrigued looks from nurses when I was walking through the hospital.

Another compulsory element of our student experience was to spend two weeks in an Obstetric Unit to gain experience in delivering babies. This could be done in any hospital of our choice. I looked at the map because I wanted to go somewhere far away. I applied to Stornoway hospital who said yes. I spent an amazing fortnight on the Isle of Lewis in the Outer Hebrides in March 1970 and delivered three babies, bizarrely all in the same 15 minute period. It was a case of, "Roger go to delivery room one."

Moments after that delivery a midwife rushed in and ran me to the delivery room next door where I delivered that baby, seconds after which a midwife appeared at the door saying, "Roger! Come to delivery room three."

After that hectic 15 minutes I revisited all the new mums to ensure there were no major problems. There were no further deliveries during the remainder of that fortnight.

It was always a joy to deal with pregnant mums. It is such a natural process; nature has been doing it for millions of years. My fear is that it becomes too medicalised. I could never understand why deliveries had to be done with the mother lying down. That takes away the effect of gravity which would continually passively dilate the cervix (the neck of the womb) between contractions.

The staff looked after me very well in Stornoway. One of them took me in her car on trips around Lewis and Harris. I can still see the picture – standing on the coral white sand of Luskentyre beach, the sea was turquoise with the sun shining and not a cloud in the sky and yet the hills opposite had a cap of snow set against that expansive background of endless blue. An eternal image.

Lewis and Harris had a mesmerising effect. I have been back several times since and always enjoyed the beauty of the beaches, the countryside and the hospitality.

During the long summer holidays of 1969 and 1970 I was a student in Walsgrave hospital, Coventry. I had seen this being built and watched the progress being made on the building every time I drove up to, or returned from Dundee. One particular day, when curiosity got the better of me, I walked in to the hospital, told them I was a medical student and asked if I could have a look around. The assistant matron gave me a guided tour of the floor that was about to open. I asked who should I contact to arrange my student clerkship; he suggested a name, I wrote and was accepted. So the summer of 1969 I was attached to a team of two surgeons and learned a lot, especially from the registrars. In 1970 I did a clerkship on the medical floor which again taught me a lot. I learned most from the registrars because that's who I spent most of my time with. I realised particularly how important the nurses are, not just from the amazing care they provide to all the suffering souls, but from their interaction with the patients in which they can sense deterioration or a looming problem. In that way they are the eyes and ears of the doctors who simply can't be there all the time. I learned to completely trust a nurse if they said they were worried about a particular patient.

By the time I left Walsgrave hospital as a student I had arranged to go back there for my first job after qualifying.

As finals and, hopefully, graduation got closer I realised we had never been taught how to suture a wound, so I asked the Head and Neck surgeon if he would give us a tutorial. We arranged a day and time. I went to the butchers and asked for half a dozen pigs trotters and when I mentioned what it was for he didn't charge me. Now suitably equipped, off we went to the tutorial and had an expert describe and illustrate the fundamentals of sewing a wound closed. We each practised on our trotter and he came by giving us guidance and suggestions. This was a valuable lesson which apparently hadn't been part of the curriculum.

Eager to gather as much and as varied a knowledge base as possible, I realised late on in my degree education that one of the most challenging things to understand is how to do a detailed neurological examination of a patient. I felt I had to become fluent in doing such an examination and the only way to do that was to go to a ward where that was routine. A locum position in the Neurosurgical ward became available, which I applied for. Consequently, with regular practice and expert tuition, I learnt to do a thorough neurological examination. Fortuitously, in my finals I was shown a lady who was displaying the symptoms of Multiple Sclerosis (she told me what was wrong with her, bless her!). I had to present my neurological findings and the likely diagnosis to the examiner. Thanks to my time spent in Neurosurgery, along with the sneaky prompt from the benevolent patient, I passed this part easily. By this time in my learning I was always more adept in dealing with the personal problems being experienced by the patient than I was in regurgitating the cold, abstract facts in medical textbooks.

After finals, we attended a dinner for all the class and some of the academic staff, including a number of the external examiners. Very cleverly this was arranged for the night before the results became available. This meant that everyone could relax and celebrate the end of six years of intense study and pressure. After the dinner many of us got together to play football. The men were still in their dinner jackets and the ladies were wearing their long gowns. It was a hoot! I don't know what time it was, maybe 6 or 7 o'clock in the morning, none of us had had any sleep. We were all enjoying the freedom, the early-morning sunshine and the football when a policeman arrived. He came over to us and told us that some of the local householders had objected to the noise we were making. He suggested we move to a field further away from the houses to continue our game. That was great policing.

Thankfully I passed all the final exams and the future beckoned.

I had no idea what I was letting myself in for.

OVERTIME

It is mandatory for everyone who graduates in Medicine to work in hospital for the first year after graduation. I did six months general medicine and six months surgery. The emphasis was on Cardiology in the first three months and kidney disease in the second three months of the medical stint. In the following six months it was mostly abdominal and vascular, with some thyroid, surgery. I had a hint of what was to come on my first day when I shared a lift with a lovely consultant physician.

He said, "You may not get much sleep, but it is very important that you eat regularly."

I thanked him for his advice and went up to the ward. The medical floor was divided into three wings: the acute wing for the most seriously ill patients who needed most care; a wing for those who didn't need to be in the acute wing anymore, while the third wing was for the convalescent phase before going home. There was a room on the acute wing where the doctor on call could sleep yet be immediately available to deal with a crisis.

The doctor on call had to deal with patients on the ward as well as any 999 calls, collapses and admissions sent in by GPs. It would take me about an hour to adequately deal with each patient coming into the Admissions unit. The registrar on the team would always supervise us. Getting 16 or 17 admissions while on call would be typical. The most I got in one 24 hour period was 22. One of my colleagues had 27.

He was so exhausted that he vomited. It was relentless. Every event was dramatic for the patient and cumulatively exhausting for us, the junior medical staff. Not only was sleep a rare commodity, eating was too. There was always something else to do, someone else to deal with. Getting to a meal was one thing, completing it was another.

Every doctor carried a bleep or pager. When you are first on call and your bleep went off, you could press a button that told you the location of the crisis. I still remember being part way through my pudding one day when my bleep went and the crash team had to run to the convalescent ward. A lady had gone into cardiac arrest; her heart was still beating but way too rapidly to function properly. It's called ventricular fibrillation. I remember it's the only time I've ever intubated someone nasally. (Intubation is passing a tube into the breathing passages so that oxygen can be given to the patient effectively). The resuscitation was effective, and we had to take her around to the acute ward for more intensive monitoring and care. It fell to me to tell her husband. I remember the patient was in her mid-thirties and had children. I told her husband what had happened and that she wasn't out of the woods yet. I explained why we had to move her and that we couldn't promise any outcome. I remember his tears. I went back to the dining room and my pudding was still on the table three hours later.

She was discharged fit and well after a three week stay.

I was at my least competent when I was exhausted. For 'least competent' read 'dangerous'. I started on the ward at 08:30 on a Friday. I got no sleep Friday night, Saturday was just as busy and I got no sleep then; Sunday was equally crazy. Not only was I sleep deprived, I wouldn't have had much food either. I eventually got to my bed on the acute ward at 2 or 3 o'clock on the Monday morning. Through the night, the Charge Nurse came in showing me a cardiac tracing on a patient. I waved it away and said it would be okay and went back to sleep immediately. He came in again on three further occasions each time brandishing cardiac tracings. I could not get out of bed. I was beyond exhausted. He said he would report me for ignoring his requests. I still could not get out of bed. I managed to get up to join the Registrar and Consultant on the ward round the next morning. The Registrar greeted me with the words:

"Roger, your masterly inactivity is exactly what Mr (let's call him Smith) needed. He is still alive this morning."

The cardiac tracings had been fixed onto the desk at the nursing station. I looked at them and thanked my guardian angels. The conventional management at that time was to give a local anaesthetic by injection and give some more of that anaesthetic slowly in a drip into a vein – a technique that has since proved to be of no value. But at the time that was the standard procedure.

How can anyone expect a fellow human being to function anywhere near normally, let alone effectively, when they are so lacking sleep and basic nourishment?

Compassion and faith in humanity are reignited when a Nursing Sister sees you in this state, commands you to sit down then brings you tea and toast, and will not allow you to leave until it is all finished. That five-minute oasis in which someone is doing something *for* you is precious, scarce and profoundly appreciated. Someone cares, someone sees you, someone helps. Then it is back to the incessant demands. Don't get me wrong, it is not the fault of the patients but of the system and the organisation. The patients and their families are experiencing life-changing events.

When I hadn't been on call and had managed to have a good night's sleep, I would go on to the ward the next morning and watch my drained, pale, exhausted colleague shuffling off the ward, hopefully to get to bed or at least have a shower before coming back to the coalface.

I remember having a meal back in the doctors' residence. I sat at a table where a doctor working in Obstetrics was sitting. He looked exhausted. He was part way through his meal when his bleep went off. He didn't stop eating, he simply took his bleep out of his pocket and dropped it into the full water jug.

Another memorable occasion involved the Senior Registrar. He had had an exhausting day and night and we had just finished a ward round the next morning when we headed down to the staff lounge for morning coffee.

He said to the group of four or five of us, I think including a consultant, "You'll have to excuse me," and he proceeded to take his shoes off. Then stood up on the table, held his arms out wide and bellowed, "AAAaaargh! …Thank you, I needed that."

There must have been at least a hundred of us in the coffee lounge at that time. The silence and astonishment were immediate. That lovely guy went on to become a consultant in a nearby city.

From this distance I can see that what we were exposed to was slavery, and we were the slaves.

Get this. We could only claim overtime if we worked more than 106 hours in the week. This was not unusual.

Whenever I'd worked overtime on the building site I would get time and a half for evening and Saturday work and double time for Sunday. I remember one Saturday in 1966 I was at the building site in the morning, working in the Rootes car factory. It was a beautiful sunny day and the Timekeeper came along in our morning tea break and said, "I don't know what you guys are doing this afternoon, but I'm going home to watch the football. You'll all be paid."

A chorus of, "Fookin' grayt!" echoed from the lads.

So I cycled home and watched the World Cup final while being paid time and a half. Surreal! Brilliant!

The hospital overtime rate: 30% of our usual hourly rate. That is 30% *not* 130% - so less than a third of our usual pay.

I think at the time nurses worked a 37-hour week. So on occasions we would do three weeks work in the same interval in which nurses worked one.

Are you surprised I thought it was slavery?

It was only after reading the book 'This Is Going to Hurt' by Adam Kay that I completely empathised with his descriptions and realised I was probably still suffering the effects of PTSD nearly 50 years later. The physical, emotional and mental drain at the time was relentless.

When you get to the point where if you sit down you fall asleep instantly. When your bleep goes you awaken just as quickly. When you rush your food (a habit I find difficult to break even this far away from it) because you know the meal is bound to be interrupted. When you can't focus, when you feel numb, when walking is a chore then you know you're exhausted. Even talking is a bit of a challenge. Thinking develops a cardboard texture. Do I do this? Do I do that? Did I do that? What do I do now? The swirl of thoughts, possibilities, probabilities all seem to collide and compete. Decision becomes indecision becomes decision.

It changes you, your habits and probably your reaction to people. Alcohol becomes a salve. It signifies that you are not on call, nothing more is expected of you. At last you can relax, and keep relaxing, until next time.

I got married in early December 1971. Sometime later my father-in-law had some business to do in London and invited us down to spend the night there. You cannot get lost driving from Coventry to London. I was so exhausted that I did. I got lost. The heaviness in the head, not thinking straight, all conspired to make me functionally useless. We got to London eventually and went out for a meal in a traditional Polynesian restaurant. I remember being served something in a wooden bowl. I fell asleep as I was looking at it. I stayed asleep; I simply could not rouse myself. I don't remember eating or drinking anything, I just slept. I remember my wife was furious at me, not honouring her father's generosity. Her father must have thought I was a right dick. I couldn't do anything else, I just had to sleep. I was still sitting up.

I'm not sure how we managed it but over Christmas the junior doctors wrote, rehearsed and performed a couple of shows for the patients who could make it down to the performance area. That was an oasis of fun amidst the typical daily slog.

In another example of the stark contrast between real world versus the medical model, I got back to my room in the hospital at about 2am. It was Christmas Day or New Year's Eve, I forget which. My key would not turn the lock. I knew I could take a shoe off, break the glass panel in the middle of door, reach inside, and open it that way. I thought maybe there is another way. The hospital is bound to have a joiner on call. So I called the switchboard who put me through the duty joiner. I explained the situation and said just tell me what to do and I'll do it.

He said, "Oh it's complicated. I'll have to come in."

"No, just tell me what to do."

But he couldn't get to me fast enough.

So I'm waiting 20 minutes or so, he arrives, sizes up the situation, takes his shoe off, breaks the glass panel, reaches inside and opens the door. Because it was Hogmanay or whatever I gave him a large dram and we chatted. He explained the reason why he was so keen to come in, "I've been waiting for this for years. I get a minimum of two hours callout. Today is a public holiday so I get treble pay and a day off in lieu." And as doctors we were on 30%, with no days off in lieu.

As he quaffed his dram I asked him what I should do about the glass, and repairing the door and the lock.

"The glass is your problem mate but I'll give yer a hand." He helped me clear it up and indicated that the repairs could not be done until after the holidays.

In the February I shifted to a surgical team.

The six months of surgery was an awful lot easier in terms of numbers of patients coming in and the time needed. There was still the occasional need to be up in the wee small hours assisting at operations in the emergency cases, but the workload was much less than in the previous six months. The surgical boss was excellent technically as well as being a very good diagnostician.

I still have a couple of standout memories. A lady came in with a lump in her breast and was scheduled for surgery the next day if it was necessary. I phoned the boss as he requested. He said, "Roger get a 50 ml syringe and a green needle and see if you can aspirate the lump and let me know what happens."

I went to the lady and asked her to show me where the lump was. She showed me, I cleaned the skin, popped in the needle and aspirated nearly 50 ml of fluid. Throughout the procedure, the lady was looking the other way. When I had finished I hid the syringe then asked the lady to show me the lump. She felt all around the area, then felt again and again. The biggest smile grew on her face and she threw out her arms towards me as if to give me a kiss. I called the boss he told me to send the fluid to the lab and the lady could go home. That added even more delight to an ever grateful lady.

In medicine we see the most awful illnesses, dreadful outcomes and many deaths. We also get to experience many beautiful and fulfilling moments.

The boss also had patients on the private wing from time to time that we also had to monitor. At the end of my six months as a Surgical Houseman the boss gave me a cheque for £25 with a note in his own hand that read:

'Roger. Thank you for your help with my privates.'

While I was still a student in Dundee, I had asked if I could be the Senior House Officer on the ENT (Ear, Nose and Throat) ward which also had a major interest in head and neck surgery. At that time I thought I wanted to do head and neck surgery as a career. When I asked the consultant if I could do his house job he literally fell off his chair in surprise.

He said, "No one has asked me that before."

It was arranged that I would do six months in the ENT Ward and six months attached to the Neurosurgery ward.

I had already worked on the Neurosurgery ward as a student. The remaining Senior House Officer (SHO) at the time had introduced me to the habit of returning to the ward late in the evening to go around the patients just before they settle down to go to sleep. It's an opportunity to hear their concerns, their fears and to offer some reassurance, both to them and to myself. It gave me a gauge as to how likely it might be for me to have a disturbed night, unless there were new admissions.

I reflected on how ridiculous it was to be so busy in my time on the medical wards that there had been no time for this simple and valuable humanity.

Our first son was born towards the end of my time in ENT.

In the first few months of his life, a weekend on call in Neurosurgery for me meant leaving home on the Friday morning and not getting back until the following Monday evening. I realised that my son did not recognise me when I returned home from a weekend on call, to the point where he was frightened when I reappeared. That's when it hit me that the impact of hospital medicine on family life was unacceptable, and I needed to make a career change. Seeing a lovely guy called Gus, who was a couple of years ahead of me and doing Obstetrics, having to phone home every evening to say good night to his children reinforced my decision.

The emotional drain in medicine has the potential to be devastating. The doctors don't want to become depersonalised or cold and emotionally numb in dealing with patients. We have to retain our humanity and empathy. We are thinking, feeling, sensate human beings. We need the succour and support of our family to regain perspective and be nourished. Our calling must not be abused and cost us what is most important in our lives.

The facts speak for themselves. Medical doctors as a professional group have the highest rates of suicide, alcoholism and divorce. To have such a group of highly intelligent, intensively (and expensively) trained and highly motivated personnel have their lives wasted by suicide and damaged by alcohol and drugs has huge costs professionally, personally and to society. Having read more recent accounts of life as a Doctor in the NHS, I wonder why it seems that little is being done about this.

GENERAL PRACTICE

Having recognised that I needed a career change I opened the British Medical Journal. There, in the back, the position of Trainee GP in Aberlour, Speyside was advertised. I applied, went for interview and was accepted.

We were in Aberlour for one year. The area was beautiful, the people delightful. John and Jimmy, who were well-established in the practice, became my trainers. They were excellent as clinicians and lovely as people. Among their philosophies was:

"You are here to learn about people as much as you are here to learn about medicine. So if anyone invites you walking or fishing or shooting you accept, and we will cover your duties."

"This is a small community. You are stuck with them and they are stuck with you. Please remember that in everything that you do and say."

"Obstetrics is only normal in retrospect."

"Whiskies are like people, there are no truly bad ones it's just that some are better than others."

There were 14 distilleries within the catchment area of the practice. Walkers shortbread is also made in Aberlour. The products from this village are available world-wide. That is an extraordinary achievement for one small village.

I felt very nourished.

I never enjoyed shooting, although I was invited. One of my hosts commented that I was a 'safe gun' and had found out that there was plenty of fresh air around a pigeon!

My wife and I were invited fishing. I caught an 8lb salmon and to celebrate the Ghillie gave us a dram of Macallan in an enamel mug with a drop of water from the River Spey, which we were standing in, added to "release the flavour". It was one of the best drams I have ever tasted. There are times in life when something just 'hits the spot' and that was one of them. That alchemy of sunshine, scenery, peace, beauty, companionship, salmon and the dram brought a moment of perfection.

Towards the end of that exceptional year, I began to look for a place for a permanent job. After looking at several, I finally settled on a practice north of Perth. On my first night we had no accommodation so I had to stay in a hotel. I was somewhat taken aback when the partners requested that I be on call on that first night. Sure enough, in the wee small hours the hotelier knocked on my door to say there was a call. I looked at my map, but with no local knowledge, had no idea where to find the property. The hotelier had to give me directions. This was a foretaste of things to come.

A little while later we moved into a farmhouse which was so cold in winter that there was ice on the *inside* of the bedroom windows. Getting out of bed was a challenge then.

After two or three months I realised that the chemistry between myself and the two principals was not sustaining and decided to leave. We stayed with my wife's parents for a while. I was jobless but not worried. I knew something better would come up. After a couple of months, I found a vacancy in Elgin, much further north on the Moray coast. We bought a lovely bungalow and began to settle in. As with Aberlour, it was a beautiful area, with delightful people and great neighbours. Some became lifelong friends.

Unfortunately, it was not at all that way within the practice. After many months, the middle partner went away on holiday for two weeks. The senior partner's view of an equitable share of the nights on call was to tell me that I was on call for 18 out of the 21 nights. This was illustrative of a master/serf relationship and his superior attitude. When my wife was pregnant, the same partner would not let me go through to Aberdeen to be with her at the birth of our second son. I have never hit anyone in my life, but that man so very nearly had his nose plastered right across his face. In that instant I decided I was leaving but said nothing. I went through to see my wife on my afternoon off. The first thing she said was, "What is wrong?"

"Nothing," I lied.

When our new son was home I told my wife the story. A while later the University of Dundee accepted me as a lecturer in Community and Occupational Medicine. I remember I was rolling up a carpet a few days before we were due to leave Elgin when I got a phone call from the senior partner saying that something had come up, and he wanted me to do his surgeries and calls on the Monday. I thought there had to be some emergency and so agreed.

On the Monday morning I went in. Normally in the mornings the partners, District Nurse, Health Visitor and Receptionist met to discuss any particular issues. We were in the middle of this meeting when the senior partner came in wearing his tweeds and carrying a fishing rod. The 'something' that had come up was clearly an opportunity for a peaceful day by the river. He stayed a few moments then left. I *very nearly* shouted "Fuck off!!"

If I had said that I would have left there and then. As it was, I chose not to demean myself and simply carried on with the business of the day, reasoning that his karma would catch up with him one day.

When I said my goodbyes to the senior secretary/receptionist she said: "I hope you find somewhere with a more amenable working environment." She understood. I thanked her and left.

One thing my experience to date taught me was how *not* to treat a partner or potential partner.

Up to this point, four years post-qualification, I had followed a more or less conventional route. So immersed was I in the rigours of the job and the demands of a young family, that there was rarely a spare moment to stop and reflect. Despite this, I was still open to new avenues of thinking.

1976 saw me starting as a lecturer in Community Medicine at Dundee University. The department was responsible for looking at groups of people with a particular illness. This study, known as Epidemiology, investigates who gets what and where and when, hoping that this information will lead you to the how and the why. I suggested that all illness data be collected in relation to postcode, so it would be easier to recognise the presence of concentrations of illness. My thought was that if sick notes were analysed by postcode then clusters of illness could be spotted early, for instance during an outbreak of influenza. I also thought this would be useful to clinicians and patients to be able to locate the top 10 illnesses in a particular postcode and also for the top 10 illnesses associated with the patient's workplace postcode.

I could also see that storing information in relation to postcode could have potential application for the Police and Commerce.

This may be common practice now, but back in the 70s, the idea was innovative. Once I had had the idea, I worked closely with a computer whizz and then presented the idea to the Professor.

The Prof said we would need to do something simple to prove that it worked so I went to Edinburgh to look at death certificates for breast cancer in Arbroath.

I graphed the results as histograms and although I can't recall the exact detail, I remember noticing some semblance of a pattern emerging from the data. I took the graph to the Senior Lecturer and explained what I had done; he looked at it and said, "Bingo! Come with me."

We presented the findings to the Professor who asked me some questions and thought it worthy of future work. Sadly, due to economic reasons I had to leave the post. Annual inflation was about 25% at the time and I was on a fixed salary. Managing our family finances was becoming a real issue. Even though I hadn't had chance to delve more deeply into the medical data, at least I felt I'd contributed something valuable in my short time in the post.

One day, shortly before I left, I walked into Dr Philip James' office (he was Senior Lecturer in Occupational Medicine) and noticed several journals open. I glanced at them and one photograph in particular caught my attention. It was a photograph of the back of the eyes of a deep sea diver. I immediately noticed that the optic discs looked to be paler in the medial halves (ie closest to the nose) and I remembered that this is a particular feature of Multiple Sclerosis. I mentioned this to Philip, who specialised in Hyperbaric Medicine, which at that time was exclusively used for divers. He remarked that that was a useful observation and went on to develop the idea further. Since that time, around 65 Hyperbaric centres have opened around the UK to treat people with Multiple Sclerosis.

A turning point was to emerge in my next role, when an old classmate from University told me of a vacancy in a general practice in Staffordshire. It was single-handed but four other single-handed GPs in the same area cooperated to be on call for all five practices one night a week until 11pm and then handed night calls and weekends over to the Deputising Service. He was one of those GPs. I discussed it with my wife and, after lecturing for 18 months, we decided to give it a go. We moved yet again, and I began the next phase of my work in Hednesford.

It was a mining area. Guys would come in with sore backs. The only thing I knew was to advise hard beds, give them painkillers and sign them off work. The same miners would come back later in the week, having made a curiously speedy recovery, and ask to be signed back to work again. They told me they had been to 'a man around the corner' who fixed their back. The man in question wasn't medical but was obviously more successful than me. I felt I had to learn what this man knew.

As so often is the case, this curiosity was soon to find an outlet. I had gone to Walsgrave Hospital in Coventry to brush up on my Obstetrics. I was doing an antenatal clinic with a doctor there who asked me one day if I was interested in attending the lunchtime meeting on Osteopathy. I went along with an open mind and was immediately fascinated. 'So this is how the miners got better,' I thought. I persuaded the presenting doctor to do a class once a week for two months if I could get some others interested. Half a dozen of us took the course on the Fundamentals of Spinal Manipulative Medicine. This gave me the basic skills in Osteopathy, which enabled me to treat the miners much more successfully than I had done previously.

Although I was finding fulfilment at work during this time, things were not going quite so well in the family. My son had really enjoyed school in Scotland yet was not doing well at the local primary school. They were using a completely different learning system, which was in vogue at the time and it was a foreign language to him. He couldn't read the textbooks.

The headmaster would not change anything, plus the class teacher was going through a nervous breakdown. We soon realised that if our son was to have any chance at progressing with his education, we had to move school. My wife came up with a brilliant suggestion: if we were going to move anyway, why not go back to Scotland.

NEW TECHNIQUES

I came to Newburgh, Fife in 1980 and began as a local GP on May 1st that year.

My philosophy as a GP was that I should give people what they needed, not necessarily what they wanted. Clearly this had not always been the case in the practice. There was a lot of antibiotic resistance in the population, and a lot of diazepam was being given out on repeat prescription. I suggested to my partner that instead of just continue in the pattern of repeating these prescriptions we interview those patients and see how essential their medication was. In the majority of cases it was deemed no longer necessary. Soon we began to supervise the withdrawal, reducing dosage and seeing those patients once per week. I guess this approach was not wholly appreciated by the patients who, unable to get their head around the correct pronunciation of my surname, settled on 'Mel-hellish'. (Perhaps this has been counterbalanced since by the nick-names 'Dr Magic', 'Dr Spock' and 'Dr Einstein', as well as the previously mentioned 'Witch-Doctor'.)

Fortunately, there were some who could see the sense in it. A few years later as I was walking along the High Street, I remember someone shouting, "Hey Doc. You were right about the Valium. It said so in the Sunday newspaper."

I wondered then if I would be more effective if I just wrote a column in the newspapers rather than seeing patients face-to-face!

With the agreement of my partner, we set up the Newburgh and District Health Club. We arranged a meeting in the town hall for those interested and asked them what they would want to see in their health club, and how they would like it run. All of the suggestions were incorporated and it ran for more than 6 years. Another thing we set up was a meeting time in the surgery for those who had heart disease. Those who attended called it, perhaps inevitably, the Lonely Hearts Club. They met once a week. The idea was to give them more confidence and encourage exercise and to change their nutrition. They used their pulse rate to control their degree of exercise. Those who had had heart surgery were able to talk to those who were waiting for the same procedure and encourage them by example and their experience.

The one part of General Practice I felt a visceral dislike for was vaccination. I could not help but wonder what we were actually doing to these babies. These little bundles of perfection. Was it really necessary to fill them with all these vaccinations?

What I did find enormously satisfying was putting the Osteopathy work I'd been introduced to at Walsgrave into practice. For a doctor, there's nothing like seeing someone come in with a symptom and walk out without it. I decided I would go to the British Association of Manipulative Medicine courses held in London one weekend per month for the winter months of two successive years to hone my skills even more. During the second year of the course, I asked the most empathic instructor if I might spend a week with him watching him work. He agreed so when the courses had finished, I spent a week in Brighton watching a master at work. I learned his system. It has stood me in great stead ever since.

As a lecturer I had become increasingly aware of the impact of tobacco on heart disease and cancer. So many patients in the practice were smokers and they needed help to break this terrible addiction. When I read that Eric Clapton come off narcotics using a new technique, I wondered if that same technique might be useful for nicotine withdrawal. I phoned an acquaintance in the pop industry to ask who managed Eric Clapton. I then phoned this manager's office and outlined my interest. 48 hours later they called me back and told me about Dr Meg Patterson, the inventor of this new technique. I phoned Dr Patterson who told me about her pioneering work with Neuro-Electric Therapy (NET).

Curious to find out more, I phoned Dr Patterson when I was in London on one of the manipulation courses to ask if I could come and see her. She said "No". Now I'm not one to be deterred when I have my heart set on something, so decided to overlook this inconvenient two letter word. I took the train down to Haywards Heath and got a taxi from there. I knocked on the door of an imposing mansion, where she was doing treatments, and asked to see Dr Patterson. When we met I introduced myself and she said rather (and unsurprisingly) curtly, "I told you I wasn't available."

"I know," I replied. "But I'm here now. I have a train to catch back to Scotland in a couple of hours so I can't stay very long."

She graciously let me in.

What she told me staggered me.

She had developed NET in Hong Kong. Solely using her technique, all craving in addiction can be stopped in four days, with no cold turkey in most cases. In six days, cocaine and heroin addiction are completely reversed, to the point where metabolically the body is in the same place biochemically as it was before narcotics were taken. For example, liver function tests become normal. What is more, the treatment does not involve pharmaceuticals. All that is needed is for the client to carry a pocket-sized device which gives particular electrical frequencies with specific waveforms via cables to contacts stuck to the bony lumps behind the ears, (called 'the mastoid processes'). These contacts are worn 24 hours a day throughout the treatment time.

I asked if it could be used for nicotine and tobacco because that was my interest and was told there was no reason why not; however she hadn't worked out the necessary frequencies and waveforms yet.

I asked if I could talk with any of the clients to get first-hand appreciation of the technique and its effectiveness. She said no, so this time I complied. I thanked her, said goodbye and returned to London for the sleeper home.

That was in 1982. The management and treatment of addicts since that date has changed little, and I find that shameful. That NET is not in widespread use in 2020 is testament to the pillorying power of Big Pharma, and the closed minds of a supine medical profession and of passive gutless governments.

The costs of addiction to society are extraordinary. 10 years ago I phoned every Chief Constable in Scotland and asked about crime rates. Each one said the same, that 60-70% of non-violent crime was to feed an addiction. What is the cost to the nation of the Police time, and the Court time? And back then cost of keeping someone in prison was £45,000 per year.

You, the taxpayer, has to pay for all these costs.

It's time that the medical profession and society woke up and demanded better treatment for addicts: they are still people.

Back in Newburgh I was having more success with people with back, neck, shoulder, arm and leg pains to the point where their relatives or friends, who lived beyond Newburgh, would ask if I could see them because they had such problems. That meant I would have to charge them, which was a totally new concept to me. I had no idea what to charge. I think my first fee to a client was £12.

I would see them after the end of the evening surgery.

I enjoyed trying to explain to the patient why they had the symptoms they had, as far as I understood it. Then the realisation dawned that my understanding wasn't as deep as I hoped it would be. We had been taught a lot about signs and symptoms but I had no great depth of knowledge about causes. The focus was on one bacterium or one virus, as if that was the sole culprit. There had to be more, but I didn't know what the 'more' was.

Regarding the back pains: I started to see people whose muscle spasm was so intense that no manipulation was possible. That sparked a thought in my mind:

'I wonder if acupuncture would be of any value here?'

For maybe only the fourth time in my life I was leafing through the adverts in the British Medical Journal. There I saw an advert for a week-long Advanced Acupuncture Techniques workshop, to be held in Liverpool by Doctors Julian Kenyon and George Lewith.

I phoned to speak with Julian Kenyon, explained that I hadn't done any acupuncture of any sort, but would really like to come on this course. He told me that would be no problem, he would send me the notes of the Introductory Course and said I had to experience 'dechi', the sensation when an acupuncture needle makes proper contact with the acupuncture point. I phoned a colleague who had been to China to learn acupuncture and he very kindly needled a specific point (LI11) on my left arm so I was able to experience 'dechi'.

Preparation complete, off I went to Liverpool. It was to be a game changer. The expansion of my knowledge, and the window into a whole new vista of diagnostic and therapeutic approaches, opened wide. There were many stand-out moments. One technique they taught was the ACR, or Auriculo Cardiac Reflex, which enables you to detect a change in the position of a wave in the pulse (NB this is also known as Nogier's Arterial Reflex, or Vascular Autonomic Signal, or VAS). Thankfully I 'got' that straightaway; some people couldn't get it at all. It was something you had to just get a feel for – no amount of intellectualising would make it any clearer. In fact, being too cerebral about it just got in the way.

I think it would be incredibly valuable if every medical professional was taught to detect and use this reflex, as it gives very accurate and immediate bio-feedback. I still use it to this day. It is one of the most useful things I have ever learned.

At that workshop I was asked to see a lady whose main symptom was joint pains, present for 10 years and which did not seem to respond to any conventional treatment.

George and Julian had developed a test for food intolerance in which an item of food was sellotaped onto a plastic paddle. Having established a reliable ACR I tested the lady for food intolerances by holding one of these paddles in her body energy field, about half an inch above the bare skin of her forearm, and detecting any change in the ACR. Absolutely everything I put on the paddle reacted. I went to find George and told him my findings. He came back to the patient with me and repeated the test on the other arm while I felt the ACR on her opposite arm. I had forgotten to test the empty control paddle against her. Surprisingly, this also produced a positive result. The conclusion what that she was reacting adversely to the plastic itself. George indicated a set of Miller dilutions designed to desensitise the patient and switch off the ACR reaction. Using the same technique, I selected that dilution, I gave her a couple of drops of that under her tongue, said I would leave her for a few minutes and come back to check how she was doing.

When I went back she was in tears. When I asked her what was happening, she replied, "For the first time in 10 years I don't have any pain. I don't have any pain ..." Her relief was palpable.

My eyes moistened as I stood there, seeing and sensing her relief. I realised I had glimpsed an extraordinary breakthrough in the potential of medicine, and it wasn't completely pharmaceutical or surgical as I had been taught.

On that course I met Roy Martina, an MD from Curaçao. We clicked. He invited me to Curaçao whenever I wished. I visited him some months later and stayed for three weeks to watch him and his team working. They introduced me to homeopathy and to Curaçao and also to Aruba. Paradise islands!

TIME FOR REFLECTION

On the flight home from Curaçao I reflected. The impression we had been given as clinical students was that osteopathy/chiropractic was dangerous; acupuncture was a weird placebo and homeopathy was utterly nonsensical, laughable, don't even think about it.

Here I was, 11 years after graduating and had been using osteopathy for three years, advanced acupuncture techniques for a few months and now I would be going to launch into the world of homeopathy as well. Life is strange isn't it!

My ambition has always been to become the most effective doctor I can be. Medical school did not fully provide that for me. Life, an open mind and endless curiosity have provided what medical school could not. I am certainly much more engaged with learning now than I ever was as an undergraduate. I think Medicine is one of those fields in which learning, fascination and curiosity are lifelong.

The following year, 1983, Doctors Kenyon and Lewith wrote to me to say that they had moved to Southampton and had an upcoming seminar with a Doctor Helmut Schimmel, a German who had developed a new diagnostic technique. I got to know Helmut very well; he came to Scotland several times and stayed with us and I went to stay with him. As well as developing what was to become a lifelong friendship, we learned more from each other on each visit, and there were multiple phone calls between times.

Helmut was a dentist who, at the age of 41, got the nudge to go to medical school, and supported himself financially by doing dental work in the evenings and weekends to gain his medical degree. At some point in his journey he became interested in the work of Dr Reinhard Voll, who developed Electro Acupuncture in his own way, by measuring the electrical resistance on acupuncture points and other reactive points in 1958. It became known as 'Electro Acupuncture according to Voll', or EAV. Helmut learned this technique and realised 1) Voll was the only person who knew the 750 points on the body, and 2) that he felt mentally exhausted after doing this. He thought there had to be a better way. So he developed a technique which measured changes in skin resistance at only one point on the body in response to multiple different stressors which were applied in sequence.

Helmut taught this technique in Southampton and gave several advanced courses over the following years. I attended all of these courses. The beauty of this technique was its simplicity. A practitioner could build up a picture of all the toxins present in a client and of the remedies needed to bring that client back to a healthy balance. These remedies were all homeopathic. I still use this technique today. The insights it can reveal are remarkable.

After using it for a few years and coming to learn its nuances I suggested to Helmut that it be called 'Autonomic Resonance or Reflex Testing', ART. He agreed. I also suggested that Resonance was the property that linked, for instance, a virus with an organ or remedy. Again he agreed. Two years later he published a book on 'Resonance Homeopathy.'

In 1985 I phoned Roy Martina and told him he *had* to learn Helmut's technique; he took that suggestion to heart. In 1988 Roy hosted a five-day workshop in Energetic Medicine in Curaçao, with delegates from 11 nations. The principal lecturers were Dr Helmut Schimmel, Dr Helmut Saure, an MD and pharmacist, Professor Gunther Heim, a Physicist from the University of Heidelberg, and Dr Roy Martina. It was a memorable event, not least because I had a one-on-one chat/tutorial with Gunther Heim sitting on the sand in the sun while we each enjoyed a beer – a great way to learn!

Back at home more and more people from beyond our practice area wanted to come to see me, so I arranged to see these clients at home in between and after my commitments in the Newburgh Surgery. The more I did, the more I learned, and the more effective I became.

My dear friend Harry and I first met in April, 1989 at a conference in Starnberg, Bavaria in South Germany. Curiously that is also the time that I first met Cyril Smith, author of 'Electromagnetic Man', who has become a great thinking partner and collaborator over the last 4 years

Ostensibly the week-long seminar was about an instrument called the BICOM. It sounded interesting so I had registered to attend months before the Spring date. Six weeks before the due date for that conference an interesting tussle was happening within me. It was a conflict between my head and my heart, between my logic and my intuition.

My head said: "I don't need to go, I don't really want to go, so I'm not going." My heart said: "You've got to go."

This tussle went on for weeks. Ultimately I gave in to my heart, thinking that the insistence of my intuition meant that I really need to get this BICOM machine. Little did I know.

Anyway, off I went.

At the first session I was sitting alone at a table and this tall slender gentleman of Indian extraction sat next to me. I instantly felt a connection. We got chatting and over the week the connection simply strengthened. His name was Harry, he was a medical doctor and was practising only non-pharmaceutical medicine in Trinidad. We swapped contact details and have been in regular contact ever since, to the point where I see Harry as a spiritual brother. He extended an invitation for me to go and visit him in Trinidad. I went in the following autumn.

We spent weekdays in his office starting around 08.30 and sometimes not leaving till 1 o'clock the next morning; he was seeing an insane number of patients. I learned a lot and we shared many concepts and ideas. At the weekend we went to Tobago. What a place! A true tropical paradise island, and the Kariwak Hotel is one of my favourite places on the planet. We took a boat out to the Nylon Pool. I got into the water and swam for a while then came back to Harry and I said, "This should be called the Silk Pool, the water is silky and silk is a natural substance just as this water is natural, not artificial like nylon."

Harry agreed but said I was too late, the Nylon name had stuck. I didn't know this then, but I would go on to contribute to an annual seminar held at Kariwak and arranged by Harry, which was based on health, spirituality (no, not religion, but the spiritual aspects of unwellness) and health. We did this for a decade.

At one point during my trip, I decided I needed to meditate. Back in Scotland I had been working the crazy hours that was demanded of GPs then, and since 1982 had been seeing some patients privately for Osteopathy, Acupuncture and latterly for Vega testing (the versatile system for getting immediate feedback from the body that I had learned from Dr Helmut Schimmel). I knew I could not continue at that rate. I had to make a decision: would I stay in the National Health Service or would I leave to follow my own fascinations and trust that I would generate enough to support my family and home.

The NHS 'package' came with the crazy working hours, working within very restrained and confined parameters yet great security and a very good pension. Yet the whole ethos seemed to be aimed at suppressing symptoms, not identifying the causes of illness.

Working privately enabled me to spend my time looking for the true causes of illness and symptoms, and helping the patient understand that they were in control; they had choice. There was zero security and no pension, yet great fascination and amazing fulfilment.

BIG DECISIONS

I decided to set myself afloat in the glorious, expansive waters of the Nylon Pool. It would provide the perfect environment for my meditative enquiry.

Before I got in, I quietly stated that I needed guidance on whether I should continue in the Health Service or leave and be a private doctor. I lay on my back in this beautiful water, blue sky, lovely sunshine and warmth, closed my eyes and went into my own time and space. After a good long while I heard a deep, sonorous, velvety male voice say to me, "Be not afraid. Be not afraid."

I came out of my reverie and heard, way in the distance, Harry's voice shouting, "Roger! Roger!"

I looked back at the boat to see that it was maybe 600 yards away, way in the distance. That's how far I had floated. I waved and swam towards the boat while it came towards me. Safely aboard we returned to dry land and went back to Kariwak.

I knew what I had to do when I got back to Scotland. I discussed it with my wife who was immensely supportive and understanding. On May 1st 1990, exactly 10 years after starting my current role as a family GP in the NHS, I started working on my own in full-time private practice. It was like stepping off a precipice wearing a parachute and hoping that it would open. It has worked so far!

Reassurance soon followed in the very welcome flow of patients. The results in terms of patient benefit, led to many word of mouth recommendations. I never had to advertise and was kept busy. The fulfilment followed.

Unfortunately, at home it was not such plain sailing and in 1995, my wife and I separated. It led me to reflect deeply about connection.

We all need connection. We all need a sense that those close to us in life are important to us and, probably, that we are important to them too. These feelings are part of that glorious, indefinable entity called love. I may be alone if I am sitting in the middle of the Sahara, yet if I feel loved I cannot feel lonely because I have that deep sense of connection. If I do not feel that deep sense of connection I can be in the middle of a busy family and feel profoundly lonely. That is heart- achingly painful.

Love and hate cannot coexist. When someone hates they cannot love. Consequently, what they give is mechanical, bereft of connection, and always tainted by the hatred and underlying anger. It is revealed in the quality of their laughter, which always sounds forced and edgy rather than spontaneous and free. When this hatred is long-term, implacable, unchangeable, the reduction of connection is continuous and corrosive. Over a decade it is destructive. I experienced this.

The emptiness of feeling unloved is a mixture of iciness, cruelty, incomprehension, bewilderment, grief. The loneliness is absolute.

Where that continuing level of anger and rage exists, there is little space for love. The aching emptiness of my early childhood returned. Mechanically I was catered for yet was in an emotional desert. I realised I was heading towards a massive heart attack or a profound mental breakdown. I could not go on. Something had to change. Heart-breaking though it was I realised we had to separate. She took the children and dogs and moved into a new house.

Some months later I first heard part of the rock opera 'Tommy' in which Roger Daltrey rasped the plea, "See me! Feel me! Touch me! Heal me!"

I burst into tears and sobbed. I sobbed for hours. Tears are coming to my eyes as I write this 25 years later.

Four years ago I read that loneliness is always a component in the generation of prostate problems. I had been feeling fine before reading that and suddenly the tears and sobs returned. I've had prostate problems for years.

Following the separation, mentally and emotionally I was a mess. I knew it would be a mistake to see clients while I was in this state so I waited and waited to feel better. It took seven months before I regained mental clarity. In that time I had no work so I had no income. I had now two homes and four children to support yet trusted that eventually all would be well.

Despite the intense discomfort, I had many insights during that time. One particular day, early during that period, I got a strong nudge from my intuition urging me to go to the supermarket *now*. My logical mind questioned it, but it was clear that my heart said I had to go. I drove 12 miles and went into the supermarket. It was a familiar journey. Yet this time, as I was walking through the supermarket, internally I asked myself: "Is it this aisle, is it this aisle?" And walked on until something inside me said, "Yes".

I turned and walked down that aisle. I was intrigued as I was guided past an array of saucepans! Then down to the end of the aisle where, on the left-hand side, was a display of CDs. Two thirds of the way down that display was a row with just one CD on it: Bruce Springsteen's Greatest Hits. I picked up the CD and there, on the back, I saw the words

'Human Touch'. Before this I'd had the faintest awareness of the song and somehow *knew* that I needed it. Once I got the CD home, I played that song over and over again in the coming weeks. I didn't *quite* know why I needed to hear it. I sort of got it on the mental level yet trusted that its true value would become felt by me at some stage.

Before the separation, our marriage was significantly impacted by my wife's rage at her father, her father's secretary and then at her mother. Although they lived only 30 minutes away, she would not allow our children to visit them. This went on for a decade. It got to the point where at a family wedding my daughter came running up to my wife and I and said, "A man over there says he is my grandfather …" She was right, he was her grandfather; yet no intervention, no suggestion, no cajoling from myself or from my father, whom she really respected, made any difference to my wife's attitude towards her parents. I even had all the children in the car one day with the intention of driving them to see their grandparents. My wife came rushing out to the car, demanded to know where I was going, angrily stood in front of the car and would not move until we all went back into the house. It's not easy living with all that anger, especially when it is sustained over such a long time.

My wife used to do the books which she sent off to the accountants annually. Her control of the money was absolute; I even had to ask her for some money so that I could go and buy her a birthday present one year. When a letter arrived from her lawyer itemising her demands, I took it to my lawyer at our first meeting. He read it, asked me some questions then said that, before he agreed to take me on, he would like me to see a friend of his. He made a phone call, said I could see his friend in 15 minutes and gave me directions. He sent me to an insolvency specialist! This guy gave me chapter and verse about becoming bankrupt, said I could do everything myself, yet if I needed his involvement to contact him again, wished me luck and his parting words were: "Tell your wife's lawyer to stop making such fucking unreasonable demands."

Jeez! Insolvency! Becoming bankrupt! Another shock to the system.

If I became bankrupt the fallout would be immense. The resulting tumble of thoughts was alarming. The children would have to leave their fee-paying school, (the state system had failed my eldest son; we had only one chance to educate them and if we sent one we had to send them all, so that's what we did). I wouldn't be able to afford the mortgage on their new house, heaven knows where they would end up geographically and educationally on top of the emotional turmoil they would be going through. Also, there was the business to think about (even though it was temporarily on hold). I now had an established private practice so clients knew where I was; if I sold up and moved away the cost of contacting them was too much time, energy and money.

I could see the logic of filing for bankruptcy yet at no stage did it feel even remotely acceptable. I realised that I simply had to find a way of keeping things going. I felt this was the right thing to do and trusted that all would work out eventually.

I then had to nourish me and try to figure out what it was that we were missing. Knowing that an answer would eventually come sustained me over days and weeks and months.

I have already said I couldn't work in that time; I simply wasn't in the right frame of mind.

No work, no income, just an increasing overdraft to pay the mortgage, school fees, energy bills and all the (unfamiliar!) domestic accountancy stuff. At one point I phoned my accountant to say that I could not afford to pay taxes that year, would he please arrange this. He told me I would have to pay double the next year. That was OK for me; it would be a problem for then, not for now. Thankfully he did that. He also asked me a question: how much did I earn the previous year? I truly had no idea, not even a ballpark figure, such was my lack of interest in matters financial. I thought I was on £1 a week plus all I could eat! Yes, it was my fault, my omission that I was so inept with accounts. I should have been more involved but I wasn't. I focused on client health, believing that all would flow from that. As long as we could afford our outgoings and a holiday that was enough for me.

The following time wasn't easy moneywise.

I had run out of cash one day and went to the supermarket to ask at Customer Services if they accepted credit cards. When they said "Yes!" I thought "Thank God, I can eat today". On many occasions I would follow after the lady putting the yellow price reduction stickers on the produce. On one occasion I reflected on how bizarre it was to have a medical degree and be hanging on by my fingernails to avoid bankruptcy. Another time it was my youngest son's birthday. I couldn't really afford the petrol to go and see him yet felt I had to at least see him and give him something. I knew he liked carrots, bought a bag of organic carrots and took it to him. I'm sure I was ridiculed for it and I felt really humbled that I could not give more yet it was simply a token of the love I feel for all my children. I can survive embarrassment, and have never much cared about what others think of me as long as I am acting from a place of truth, integrity, love, compassion and honesty. That is all I endeavour to be.

Some would say that as a doctor I could have got a locum job somewhere which would have paid me good lumps of money. Technically yes, that may have been possible. Yet looked at from my perspective, it would have meant me returning to the notion of suppressing symptoms which is something I cannot accept philosophically. It is not in my makeup, plus I wasn't in the right headspace. Yes, I survived on boiled brown rice on many days, drinking the water it was cooked in to get all the nourishment out of it. Yes I *could* have done things differently but it simply didn't fit. I trusted that my inner being was guiding me and I had to stay in my integrity, no matter how uncomfortable that was at times.

Tough times, yet somehow I kept trusting that all would be well eventually.

In hindsight I think I went into my shell after the concept of threatened bankruptcy. I didn't have the mental or emotional resources to even go and see my children for many weeks; I felt too raw.

Seven months after the separation I began to feel very unwell. For two or three days I couldn't eat but slept a lot. Then it started: I got hotter and hotter and hotter, yet did not sweat at all. On the fourth or fifth day I was burning up, but still not a bead of sweat appeared. At the peak of my unwellness and hotness I realised deeply what it was that we were missing in the marriage.

My wife and I simply had not made enough time for each other. We each thought we were doing the right thing. She was running the house and seeing to the children's needs while I was focused on my work and creating revenue to support us. In retrospect we should have made more time for just each other, and reinforced it with more human touch. We needed more 'us' time. So simple. So fundamental. So essential.

Then, back with the reality of my unrelenting fever, I was faced with a huge white wall. My heart was thumping, I had never felt so hot. This white wall was right in front of me. My intuition told me that I had a profound life-changing choice to make. Conceptually, I was facing a decision to 'turn left' or 'turn right'. If I turned left in front of this wall I would be heading straight towards that massive coronary or profound mental breakdown.

I felt I was on the edge of death.

My inner Being 'knew' that if I so much as lifted a stethoscope or a thermometer, or even counted my pulse, that I would be 'turning left'. Yes, I had to completely ignore the conventional approach to my state. I knew I could only turn right, not knowing what would happen yet I trusted, I completely trusted that it would lead to a much better outcome. I laughed at myself and at the position I was in. Humour is such a saviour.

I called this episode 'the Volcanoes'.

I was virtually drained of energy and slept for the next two days, to be woken by a friend who came in. I saw the look of shock and horror on her face when she first saw me. I felt bad, I guess I looked bad, though I'm sure I would have looked very much worse 48 hours before. I tried to get up and scarcely had the energy to walk. Everything slowly improved over the next few days yet major exertion was beyond my reach until eventually that improved too.

As mentioned, this was seven months after we had separated. I phoned my wife and asked if we could meet. She agreed and we arranged to see each other the next day. I told her that I had found an answer as to what we needed, and it was so simple. I asked her directly if we could get back together again. With an air of irritation, she commented that I was only asking her this now because her boyfriend had only just moved in to stay with her in her new house the day before. Genuinely, I was totally unaware of this event. I did my best to reassure her that it had nothing to do with him, but it was just about us. She said, "No". I thanked her and left.

The divorce went ahead.

I came to realise that love doesn't stop; it changes its texture. That you can't live with someone doesn't mean to say you don't love them.

A few days later I started seeing clients again. Something really curious happened in the first two days of resuming consultations. Two unrelated people at different times on the first day said to me:

"You realise that your wife didn't believe in what you are doing, don't you?"

This was replicated on the second day by another two people, again unrelated, and at different times of day. I was astonished. I had no idea. I thought she had always been very supportive.

Since then I take much less for granted and ask lots more questions.

So here I was with a colossal overdraft, clarity about the marriage and resuming the medicine that still fascinated me.

Later, in the December following our separation, I had a beautiful surprise: my ex-wife invited me to her house to have Christmas dinner. I went along, rang the doorbell, my youngest greeted me and we were walking up the stairs. Halfway up, my eldest came down, greeted me and said, "Dad, you're not wanted here." That hurt, deeply. I said, "But it's Christmas, the season of goodwill to all men".

"I'm sorry Dad but ..." I turned, went downstairs and out to the car. My wife's partner couldn't face me himself so he sent my eldest in his place. I returned home. I fasted and reflected, didn't even turn on the TV and read a book instead. That's how I spent many Christmases after that.

Several years later, when I realised that a lot of the residue of my personal pain was still unresolved, I wondered whether I would benefit from some counselling. I saw a couple of counsellors yet somehow wasn't impressed. So one day, sitting at my desk in my consulting room, I threw my hands up into the air and said, "Okay God, if you think I will benefit from counselling, I leave it to you to provide the best, most appropriate form of counselling for me," then I forgot all about it.

Forty-eight hours later I had a telephone call from a lady I hadn't spoken to for at least fifteen years. She was talking on the phone and while she was talking, the message kept crossing my mind, 'Ask her about counselling, ask her about counselling …" So I did.

She recommended somebody and gave me their contact details. I called that person who told me about something she was involved in called Life Training (now called 'More to Life'). I asked if she could put me in touch with somebody else who had been through the same course, which she did. As soon as I phoned about it, I knew something felt right. I mulled it over for a day or two then phoned back.

I went to the extended weekend course, which was facilitated by a remarkable lady called Briggy. Within minutes of her working with me, in front of the group, I was sobbing. I had suppressed so much around the attempted suicide at 6 years old, on top of all my recent woes, and here I was sobbing it out in buckets. That was transformative. The whole weekend for me was releasing, energising, life enhancing, life affirming.

I was in a really curious place driving home. I had a powerful car, the beckoning motorway was empty at 2 o'clock on the Monday morning; the temptation was to really let the car sing, yet I was at peace and 60mph felt more than adequate. During the journey I reflected on the weekend. It felt as if I'd had ten years of counselling in the previous 55 hours. It was rejuvenating.

I've come to believe that the Universe, or God, or whatever name you give to the mystery, is always supportive, and He, She or It will find a way to provide exactly the understanding, lesson or reassurance you need.

MY LESSON IN ACCEPTANCE

In January 1997 I was in the middle of a consultation with a client and my phone rang. It was my eldest son, "Dad, I don't want you to worry, but Rorie (my youngest son) is just being put into an ambulance. He was hit by a car ..."

I asked a few simple questions, asked him to give my love, and told the client that I had to terminate the consultation.

I knew that my son was too far away for me to be there before he went into the operating theatre. So I sat and meditated, asking what I needed to do right now that would be of most value. What came to consciousness quite quickly was very simple. I needed to absolutely accept whatever the outcome was, whether that was death or perfect health or anything in between. I did that. That acceptance was total; it was complete and utter acceptance of the outcome. I really have no idea how I was able to access that state in such extreme circumstances.

Then I noticed something curious; I had zero anxiety. I pondered that for a few moments and realised that with complete acceptance, there is no need for anxiety in any form. That was incredibly releasing and freeing.

I telephoned two dear friends, both very sensitive and aware, on different sides of the world. Despite the time difference they both took my call, expressed their feelings and promised to call me back. After their contemplation they phoned back to say they felt the outcome would be favourable. That was reassuring and yet neither added nor subtracted from my complete acceptance of the circumstances and the as yet unknown outcome.

During the time of their contemplations, I meditated. I asked what I can do from this distance that would be of maximum benefit to my youngest son. Silently I began to send love to every member of the NHS staff who were involved in my son's care, however directly or indirectly. Along with the outflowing of love, I sent a silent request that they work at 100% of their capabilities. This was directed towards the ambulance staff, the Accident and Emergency staff, the operating theatre staff, the surgeons, anaesthetists, all the medical staff, all the nursing staff, all the ward secretaries, the administrators, the cleaners, the telephone staff. In short, everybody who contributed in whatever way to his care.

His mother was with him so I said I would go in overnight to be with him. Meantime, I calmly went about the rest of my day, and cooked myself an evening meal before heading off to the hospital to sit with Rorie.

It is difficult to emphasise the complete lack of anxiety. I think until anyone has experienced that total level of acceptance that the notion of zero anxiety in such a circumstance is unreal, unnatural maybe even cold and unfeeling. In my experience it is none of these things. Love was pouring through me towards my son, untainted by any particle of fear. I was relaxed and loving. I felt calm, gentle yet giving.

I went to see him, spoke briefly to him, kissed him and let him sleep. I sat in the chair beside his bed. I was in the lotus position and meditating, bringing down love and healing towards him. I didn't care what anyone else thought; this was my son, and I felt I was adding to his healing. Anyone else must have looked at me and thought I was nuts. I didn't give a damn.

I realised that he was still experiencing pain despite his morphine drip. I took acupuncture pins in with me on my subsequent visits and popped them in as appropriate. To this day he says that this helped. I also gave him some homeopathics to reduce shock and contribute to healing.

After brilliant surgery and great anaesthesia, wonderful nursing care and terrific physiotherapy, he made a beautiful recovery. Two years later he was playing full kit American football for the Scottish under 18's despite being only 16 years old. A wonderful example of our tribal resilience and 'nothing will get in my way' attitude; he did this despite previous compound fractures to elbow and ankle, where he was close to losing his foot, and having multiple orthopaedic and plastic surgeries.

The wisdom of the Oriental Ancients is to accept unconditionally and be unattached to outcome. I have now lived and experienced that wisdom, and feel deeply blessed by such unexpected gifts of reassurance.

I was to experience a similar gift of reassurance in a completely different way in 2006, when my brother Adam and sister-in-law Pauline had been staying at their house in Scotland. Pauline's mum became ill and was taken into hospital. One day I offered to accompany them on a visit to the hospital . When we got there she was sleeping and barely rousable. Pauline saw that her mum's water jug was empty so picked it up and took it away to refill it. The instant Pauline left the cubicle her mother sat up, turned to face me, looked me straight in the eyes and said:

"We are very pleased with what you are doing you know, you must carry on". Then she said it again: "We are very pleased with what you are doing you know, you must carry on."

Then she lay back on the bed, closed her eyes and resumed her semi-comatose state .

I stood stock still with tears running down my cheeks. Then Pauline returned.

Perhaps I thought she wouldn't believe me, maybe I didn't want to distress Pauline but, for whatever reason, I didn't even tell her what had happened until two years after her mum died.

Later during the visit, in an anguished whisper, her mum said, "Get me out of here, Rog. Get me out of here."

A few days later they arranged to have her taken back to their home in Coventry where she died peacefully some 3 weeks later.

That experience in the hospital was a welcome reinforcement and reassurance for me that I was on the right track.

My spiritual teacher Derek O'Neill had taught us about the 'Bardo', the Tibetan word for the phase between death and ascent. I find Derek's perceptions, findings, insights and abilities astonishing (and all with no bullshit). Regarding the Bardo, he had mentioned that it was possible to help those who have just died by repeating a simple mantra every day 'Om mane padme hum' for 49 days. He also said that for the first three days immediately after death, the deceased do not realise they have died.

When I heard that my ex-wife had died very suddenly in 2015, even though we'd been apart for 20 years, I felt it appropriate for me to start the daily mantra for her Bardo.

One late evening, I was sitting on the end of my bed about to get undressed. I was sitting gazing out through the window into the garden when the clearest essence and vision of a beautiful lady came into the room wearing an inky blue matching blouse and skirt. She looked me straight in the eye and gave me the softest gentlest kiss on the lips. In that instant I knew that she fully understood me, perhaps for the very first time, and that everything between us was resolved and beautiful. I felt the sense of her as she brushed past my right shoulder and left. I knew with certainty that it was my ex-wife. It was the third day after her death.

The peace that that kiss brought me was profound and stays with me.

I continued doing the mantra every day for the next 46 days.

Having curiosity and an open mind has proved to be endlessly rewarding. I keep learning more every day, which I put into practice both personally and professionally. That said, the line between these seems almost non-existent now. I see the whole of life as an experiment in which we don't know the answers, but we know the eventual outcome. What we haven't a clue about is the path we are going to take to get there.

What continues to be fascinating is how much I don't know. It is humbling and fills me with wonder.

Bear with me and I'll tell you a curious wee story.

In 2006, two dear friends, Gunnar from Norway and Bernadette from California, wanted to see some of the UK's renowned historical sites – Glastonbury, Avebury, Stonehenge, and Salisbury cathedral. They came to stay with me in Scotland and after a few days recovering from jetlag we went on our journey.

In Glastonbury we had arranged to meet someone who was very helpful in showing us around. We watched the sunrise from the top of the Tor and, before leaving for the stone circles our guide suggested that we see Avebury as the cathedral and Stonehenge as a parish church. We thanked him and went on our way.

We saw what he meant and I think we were all disappointed by Stonehenge. On the lookout for something a little more inspiring, we headed off to Salisbury cathedral. While Bernadette and Gunnar were doing the tourist thing with their cameras, I was just the chauffeur and gopher and so was simply ambling around in the cathedral with no particular thought in mind. I was attracted to the stained glass window behind the altar and walked towards it. When I was some 20 paces from the altar I inclined my head, out of respect, towards the gold cross in the centre of the altar and into my right ear came the words:

"The divinity you are bowing to is you. The divinity you are bowing to is you."

I stood absolutely still. I was stunned. Tears rolled down my cheeks. Tears of joy, of gratitude. Bernadette saw me, asked what had happened and, after I told her kept saying "Oh my God, oh my God!".

The message I got in the Nylon Pool was 'Be not afraid. Be not afraid.'

Pauline's mum had said to me "We're very pleased with what you are doing you know, you must carry on." Then she said it again: "We're very pleased with what you are doing you know; you must carry on."

What strikes me as curious is that each of these messages of guidance from 'on high' is spoken twice, almost as if to confirm that I wasn't mistaken in what I was being told at the first hearing.

I guess we get the messages we need when we have 'the ears to hear'.

DEATH

Given how inevitable it is that doctors will come face to face with death, our training on the matter was inexcusably inadequate. I can only hope that it is different now. Working in hospital, once there was nothing more we could do for a patient, he or she became someone else's responsibility. We merely moved on to the next person in our relentless schedule and thought little more about it.

The only time we dealt directly with a patient and their family beyond death was if a post-mortem was required. The only advice we were given was a paltry 'Be sensitive about it'. It was just another aspect of our job that had to be done. There was no time to be emotional or philosophical about it.

As a GP, despite all the medical knowledge and resources I had access to, I have never felt as powerless or as useless as the time I was called urgently to a house to find a mother cradling her cot-dead child. He was 7 months old. I could only empathise with the parents and do what little I could to support them.

Since that time, there were many instances when I had to support patients who were dying at home and their loved ones. I began to use the Bach Flowers combination 'Rescue Remedy' finding it to be gentle and powerful. It seemed to ease the whole process and reduce the levels of anxiety and fear in the dying. I gave everyone in the household a few drops at each visit, explaining that no overdose was possible, only benefit.

In the book 'The Tibetan Book of Living and Dying' it says that the dying only need to know two things. The first is that they have permission to go and secondly that those left behind will be okay. This is why the relatives play such an important role in their loved one's passing.

My view is that everyone who is dying deserves to die at home, in the presence of their closest family. It can be made as beautiful as possible. Flowers, their uplifting music, being sung to, being read to, and making the whole process as comfortable, dignified, gentle and loving as possible. The dying need peace. So often in a hospital room filled with relatives, something curious would happen; they would all leave for a cup of tea or a meal and while they were absent, their loved one would have they peace needed and choose that time to die.

A few years ago, a lady in her mid 40s came to see.

Just the week before she came, I had had the intuitive nudge to include 'Willingness to get well' in my testing. I had thought that curious because I always assumed that everyone who came to see me wanted to get well. Otherwise, why would they come?

I had only gone 4 steps into the test when I discerned that her 'Willingness to get well" was only 20%.

At that moment I stopped the test and said to her "I am going to ask you an apparently silly question. How much do you really want to get well?"

She looked at me horrified, dropped her face into her hands, and tearfully said "I don't. I've done everything, I've been everywhere... I've had enough. I'm only doing it for my family and my husband."

She had had treatment for breast cancer – including mastectomy, chemotherapy radiotherapy – and her cancer had returned.

So, we talked about death and dying. We had quite a long conversation. She raised her thoughts and fears and worries, and we discussed them.

I told her that whatever she chose to do was right for her, and nobody had the right to challenge her decision. Whatever decision she made she had to be comfortable with.

I did say that if she did change her mind, I would be very happy to see her again and do what I could for her.

That was many years ago. I haven't seen her since.

After this, I realised I needed to ask more questions of this type and so now include the following in my assessments: What is their intention to get well? I ask this on each of the physical, emotional and mental levels.

I also ask "Is this legitimate suicide?" This is a concept that was introduced to me by Professor Gunther Heim. He stated that probably10-15% of people with cancer are committing suicide in a socially acceptable way. I didn't believe him at the time; in fact, I felt that even the suggestion was somewhat distasteful, but now I agree completely. That is what I find. There is a part of them, most often deeply suppressed, that wants out.

The Buddhists prepare thoroughly for the stages of dying and death. I wonder if it is this preparation and complete acceptance which gives them such a sense of peace. When we have complete acceptance of the inevitability of death perhaps only then can we truly seize the day fearlessly.

The Dalai Lama, when asked what surprised him most about humanity answered, "Man. Because he sacrifices his health in order to make money. Then he sacrifices money to recuperate his health. And then he is so anxious about the future that he does not enjoy the present; the result being that he does not live in the present or the future; he lives as if he is never going to die and then dies having never really lived."

I've always found it curious that we all know death is coming yet we act as if we are immortal. None of us knows when or how it will happen. We just hope it's not today.

Certainly, in the western world, we put an incredibly high value on human life. When I see the resources that are deployed in treacherous conditions to rescue souls who are in peril, to me this is a tangible example of respect for the value of life.

Therefore, I am mystified when individuals who know what they could be doing to enhance their health (like simple life-style changes) choose not to, and so speed their way to their graves. I guess that my efforts to support life have become so deeply ingrained that I have found it distinctly challenging to accept that not everyone has the same priority.

I've found that it often takes a brush with death before people change their priorities and realise how important it is to make some different choices.

Perhaps these few phrases sum up the commonly held notions of death:

- Death in old age is expected.
- Death in middle age is a surprise.
- Death in youth is deep sadness.
- Death in infancy is devastating.
- Death erases potential.

Personally, having invested a lot more time in deep contemplation on the subject, I am now deeply grateful for a broader spiritual perspective on death, and find comfort in Walt Whitman's assertion:

"Has anyone supposed it lucky to be born? I hasten to inform him or her it is just as lucky to die, and I know it."
Walt Whitman, Leaves of Grass.

PART TWO

THE MEDICINE

MOVING BEYOND CONVENTION

What you will read in this part of the book is based on the knowledge and conclusions that I have accumulated over nearly 50 years of practising Medicine. The vast majority of these are the observations gleaned predominantly from patients. As I mentioned in the introduction, I've come to rely almost completely on the profound wisdom that is held in the patient's body to ascertain what is going on within it, rather than referring to what has been recorded in medical literature.

Consider this – the objective conclusions that are reported in medical articles, academic papers or text books are based on empirical study; and in each study, the number of sample cases contributes significantly to the credibility of any findings. Therefore, all deductions arrived at through these large-scale studies can only ever be generic. They teach us about statistically significant patterns of response, which is undoubtedly useful, but they do not teach us much about individuals. Any anomalies either continue to be puzzled over or are simply discarded.

I have come to believe that *every* individual is an anomaly of one kind or another, and that my success in treating people who have not been able to regain their health through conventional routes, is because of this core belief. I also believe that the success of the methods I now use is based on my ability to see beyond three core conventions that I was immersed in during the first 12 years of my medical education. These are:

- **Convention 1** – The human body relies on a combination of mechanical and bio-chemical processes to function effectively. Therefore, the treatments most likely to be effective are a combination of surgical and/or pharmaceutical.
- **Convention 2** – The focus of medical intervention is on alleviation of symptoms. A lot of resource goes in to investigating symptoms so that a diagnosis can be sought, and the resultant diagnosis will predict the most appropriate treatment plan.
- **Convention 3** – Most chronic systemic illness e.g. rheumatoid arthritis, diabetes, hypertension gets worse over time and needs to be managed. There is an assumption that if all goes well, the condition may be successfully managed or even in remission, but it is unlikely to be completely healed.

Impressively, after our three foundational years in medical school, in welcoming the students to the clinical segment of our training, Professor Sir Iain Hill said to us:

"...Ladies and gentlemen, I have a confession to make: fifty percent of what we teach you will be wrong; I only wish I knew which fifty percent..."
(I know I have quoted this before yet it meant a lot to me and feel that it bears repetition just here).

In the years that followed, in my quest to become an ever-more effective doctor, I knew I wanted to look into that 50% that was 'wrong' either through omission or commission.

What I recognise now, is that my greatest progress started to come when I began to question the fundamental conventions. It was only by seeing that the existing model of medicine was incomplete and, at times, ineffective that I began to seek out models of health and healing that broadened my understanding and increased my effectiveness.

Over time, I was able to augment the conventional medical model with the following:

- **Beyond Convention 1** – The human body is fundamentally an energetic system. Mental and emotional states have an enormous impact on the flow of energy in the body, and are key factors in both the generation and healing of illness.
- **Beyond Convention 2** – The focus of all my interventions is on identifying causes on a case-by-case basis. No matter what the person's diagnosis, their route in to and out of their illness is unique. Treatments are always based on the immediate needs of the person and are not dependent on their diagnosis.
- **Beyond Convention 3** – I believe that all illness has the potential to be reversed, no matter what it is or at what stage. The body, in its extraordinary wisdom, knows what to do. My job is to help each person to create the right inner environment to enable healing to happen. That said, we are all going to die and I believe that it is important for a person to heal on the mental, emotional or spiritual level, even if they do not have enough time left to recover physically. Healing on these levels is just as valuable and transformative as regaining physical health at that stage.

These beliefs are the foundation to everything I now do in my practice. Throughout the rest of the book, I will do my best to explain these in more depth, sharing examples of real people who have benefitted from looking at health and healing in this way. My intention is to demonstrate that there is huge value in seeing beyond convention, and that by doing so, you will have much more awareness and more control over your own health and wellbeing.

ILLNESS – AN UNCONVENTIONAL PERSPECTIVE

What is immediately apparent as soon as we dip our toes into the subject of illness, is that the number of illnesses that human flesh is heir to is extraordinary. Yet, interestingly, the number of contributory factors that cause this complex myriad of illnesses is surprisingly few.

In other words, different diseases may have the many of the same contributory factors, yet the individual response to these factors is vastly different. Therefore, each person's expression of illness is different.

To begin to look at illness in a more personal and empowering way, and move away from seeing it as the cruel hand of fate, I'll start by expanding on the 'Beyond Convention' statements in the previous chapter.

THE BODY AS AN ENERGETIC SYSTEM

The difference between you and your corpse is energy, also called life force energy or Chi. When you run out of life force energy, there will not be enough energy available to your tissues to sustain healthy normal metabolism. The heart will have no energy to pump, the lungs will have no energy for breathing. To quote the line of a song:

"What is death but parting breath?"

The natural patterns of the flow of energy throughout the body were determined thousands of years ago in Chinese Medicine. Chinese Medicine says that in health, this energy flows in a regular pattern over 24 hours and then repeats the sequence. This continuing flow provides the energy to nourish and sustain all the processes necessary for life. Its healthy flow is dependent on the breath, good nutrition, deep relaxation and sleep.

If anyone had mentioned this to me whilst at medical school, my response would have undoubtedly been "Bullshit! What the f*** has this got to do with medicine?" Evidently, this complete dismissal is not uncommon, due to a widespread lack of understanding about energy and its impact on health. Therefore, many intelligent, rational-minded scientists assign it to the 'mystical nonsense' bucket before giving it a second chance.

If you are predominantly left-brained or are simply looking for an explanation that makes sense, may I offer a possible mechanism for the development of illness, founded on the work of German biophysicist, Fritz-Albert Popp.

Popp was able to ascertain that cells throughout the body communicate to neighbouring cells through the passage of photons. These photons have no mass and travel at the speed of light. Consequently, all cells and all systems have up-to-date information about what is happening throughout the entire body at all times.

"We are still on the threshold of fully understanding the complex relationship between light and life, but we can now say emphatically, that the function of our entire metabolism is dependent on light."
Dr. Fritz Albert Popp

When we are healthy, this information flow is continual and vigorous. Then, an event happens and those involved note the event on the mental level. Still on the mental level, that event is judged. It is assessed as good, bad, unfair, tragic, dreadful, shocking, etc.

With that judgement comes a response on the emotional level. There may be grief, anger, rage, heartache, guilt, shame, hatred, resentment and so on. When these emotions are not expressed thoroughly at the time, often due to cultural and social conditioning, their energy remains within the cells. These suppressed energies create disturbance in the system. And that disturbance provides a degree of obstruction to the healthy flow of photons.

When the habit of judging continues, so the emotional burdens build, increasing the level of disturbance in the system, and the flow of photons becomes even more impeded. This is often reinforced by each mental revisit to the triggering event because the emotions become more hardened.

There comes a point where a vigorous healthy flow of photons can no longer be maintained. The reduced photon flow leads to the downstream organs receiving less information, so disturbing their normal physiology and biochemistry. When these disturbances continue without resolution, so cellular function changes and pathology begins and keeps building over time. Eventually symptoms emerge and awareness of disease develops.

In short, **illness comes as a result of disruption to the normal, natural flow of energy in the body**. Therefore, any assessment and treatment of disease must take into account the factors which cause the disruption.

Having seen the value of looking at health in this way, I now think of illness and disease simply as disturbed energy states and aim to identify and correct those energy flows with the intention of returning the whole person to health where possible.

During an appointment with a patient in 1990, I picked up a high level of anxiety. I also couldn't help but notice that his wife looked considerably uncomfortable during her husband's consultation. On enquiry, they told me that she (let's call her Sue) had a painful swelling under her jaw that was affecting her tongue and speech and she was scheduled to have surgery in two days' time, to deal with a blocked salivary gland. This explained her husband's anxiety. I suggested that a bit of acupuncture might alleviate her discomfort. Sue said she was willing to give anything a try so I inserted a few acupuncture needles and gave her a few drops of a homeopathic tincture under her tongue. I then left her with the needles in place whilst I completed the appointment with her husband. There was no obvious change when I went back to Sue, but they were nevertheless grateful for my efforts.

Shortly after Sue arrived home, an 'eruption' took place under her tongue. She dashed to the sink and watched as blood and pus burst out. Then there was a 'clink' and amidst all the goo was a small jaggy calcium stone. Instant relief!

Sue kept her hospital appointment, and when the Surgeon examined the site he was amazed – no swelling just a small exit wound under the tongue. He was baffled as it was unusual for the stone to eject. No surgery was required. There was no further problem thereafter.

Great result! When the energy pathways were cleared, the body did the rest.

In another example, one evening, when she was 4 years old, my daughter came to me sobbing.

She said, "Daddy I did what you told me **not** to do. I ate all those sweeties all at once and now I've got this toothache."

"Would you like me to do something for you?" I asked.

"Yes please Daddy."

After detecting the necessary point, I popped a single gold pin into that point on her earlobe.

She squealed immediately and very loudly.

"Daddy, it's gone!"

How many painkillers can do that?

I've found that younger patients typically respond more rapidly to this kind of treatment.

Interestingly, the actuarial prime of life is age 13 – this is the age at which there are fewest deaths per 100,000 population. Perhaps this is one reason why teenagers have immense metabolic energy and feel indestructible. It is the strength of their life force energy which protects them from developing many conditions, despite having many of the predisposing factors to those conditions active in their lifestyle.

As the years pass, our energy gradually diminishes, and conditions which have been held in check for many years begin to appear. This happens for two reasons: the first is that the resilience of the body is less than it was several years before; the second is that the toxins, from whatever source, have been slowly accumulating and a crossover point has been reached. This point is the threshold before which resilience was enough to suppress the impact of these toxins, and after which the resilience is insufficient to combat the greater toxic burden. Thus, symptoms begin to appear as evidence of underlying dis-ease.

Another way to view the behaviour of the human body in energetic terms is to consider it akin to the ocean, with its ebb and flow, the rhythm of the waves and its continually changing character. It is possible to describe just one aspect of the ocean at any one time, e.g. by measuring the height, speed and frequency of the waves. Yet none of this explains the forces which come together to create *that* wave with *that* composition moving in *that* way, nor the impact each wave has on the whole ocean. The energetic forces impinging on the water, such as the wind, the phase of the moon, the contours of the sea-bed are all necessary to understand the whole. The nature of the ocean's character and behaviour is entirely dependent on the interaction of these different energies.

Similarly, Medicine describes the components in, and the behaviour of, tissues in illness and disease. It does nothing to explain the forces which come together to produce that illness in that tissue at that time. The energies contributing to an illness are given scant attention. This brings us neatly to the second of the three 'Beyond Convention' approaches.

IDENTIFYING CAUSES OF ILLNESS

As I've already outlined (and I'm sure you will know from your own experience), the most common approach in current western Medicine is to listen to a litany of symptoms, conduct multiple investigations, attempt to aggregate the findings to fit a recognised diagnosis, and prescribe the necessary pharmaceutical or surgical treatment in order to make the patient's life more comfortable. The result, typically, is that patient feels a little better (at least in the short term) and the medical practitioner is able to recount a reasonably detailed description of their condition.

However, a *description* of a disease, no matter how detailed, is not the same as providing an *explanation* of how it came about. It may tell the patient a lot about the 'What?' yet very little about the 'How?' or 'Why?' Also, the treatment is deemed effective if there is success in suppressing symptoms, yet this does not begin to address the 'How?' or 'Why?' There may even be an assumption that, if the patient feels better, does the 'How' or 'Why' really matter?

Evidently this has limitations.

Firstly, the patient's condition needs to be well-established before it fits into a recognised syndrome, and is therefore a reflection of prolonged tissue change. Secondly, the suppression of symptoms does nothing to address the circumstances that caused those tissue changes.

Pioneering microbiologist and chemist Louis Pasteur, whose findings were central to the germ theory of disease, apparently recognised this on his deathbed when he said:

"The bacterium is nothing, the terrain is everything."

The terrain refers to the biological environment. It is the condition of the terrain which allows infection to develop. Pasteur ultimately realised that a bacterium is only active because the body's defences are not strong enough to combat it. The real reason for the infection is some degree of compromise in the Immune System. This realisation seems to have been overlooked in much of the philosophy of modern medicine.

To offer a simple illustration: consider being in the midst of a flu epidemic. With an effective immune system, the body can shrug off the viral attack just like water off a duck's back. Or, put another way, if your raincoat is intact you cannot get wet, regardless of how heavy the rain may be.

It may also be that the number and size and shape of the holes in each person's raincoat are caused by a particular combination of physical, mental and emotional burdens. Each of these will reduce their protection, causing them to get wet in slightly different places.

It is this difference which means that while persons A, B and C may each have the same diagnosis, the reason for the holes in their individual raincoat is different in each case and the advice or treatment needed has to be individually tailored. Examining the rain won't help each individual.

I have a deep sense of disquiet each time I hear a long tale of woe from a client. They typically come to me as a last resort having been round and round countless consultants, often for many years without improvement. Such stories can still leave me feeling dismay, anger and sadness, yet I can also empathise with those involved. The massive intellect, commitment, integrity and sheer professionalism of the medical personnel and the colossal resources, are all applied in good faith. I can appreciate their own frustrations and the limitations of what they are able do given their current constraints.

HEALING IS ALWAYS POSSIBLE

I believe that **every illness acquired in life *can* be reversed or at least halted**. The only thing that cannot be reversed is death. My view is that if the body has produced it then, if the causes are accurately determined and dealt with, and healing is stimulated, the body can *un*-produce it. That is what has driven me for the last 40 years.

From my simple perspective, to HEAL is to change from an illness or disease pattern to a healthy pattern. Therefore, my aim with every client is to reset the body to its healthy settings.

This means:

- Ensuring that the energy flow in the body is normal and healthy
- Removing all toxins from the body
- Avoiding new exposure to these toxins, thus preventing recurrence
- Ensuring that the home environment supports health and healing, not illness
- Enabling them to maximise their potential as a healthy, happy, loving, joyous being who is fully engaged with life

Despite having decades of learning and experience, I can only do this successfully when the client is **fully** involved in the process. It is always a partnership. For my part I do everything I know to initiate, stimulate, progress and support healing. Regarding the clients' part, I do know that it takes great commitment and tons of discipline to achieve health, and I know this isn't easy whilst in the depths of detoxing and feeling rancid. The temptation is often to give up. To some extent, that's human nature; most of us just want an easier life. However, giving in to that temptation means that the detoxing has to start all over again because health has been pushed further away.

Commitment and discipline are vital in returning to health. If this applies to you, do you have reason enough to maintain your commitment, keep the discipline you know is important, and keep moving towards being healthy again? Because being passive is not an option. You will be doing most of the hard work, and you need to decide if it's worth it.

When you've got your health back again you have:

- More energy
- Better concentration
- A healthier appetite
- A healthy weight
- Better sleep
- Better libido
- A much more even temperament – no anxiety nor depression or mood swings
- Zero symptoms
- Zero need for treatment
- More to give

- Increased enjoyment and engagement with life. You are sparkling!
- The tendency to laugh much more easily
- The likelihood of attracting more beauty, joy and serenity into your life

Committing to your health signifies that you value, respect, appreciate and love yourself enough to invest in the only true asset you have. Your health is your greatest wealth.

In 2020 I met a man who embodied my belief that healing is always possible. He had completely recovered from a muscle wasting disease called Myasthenia Gravis, which is almost always progressive and ultimately terminal. Doesn't everyone else with that diagnosis deserve to know how, what, why, and when that happened? What did he do? What did he experience? Can we all learn from that? The fact that it happened once means that can happen again and that opportunity should be given to all with that diagnosis, wouldn't you agree? We should be investigating these radical remissions thoroughly so that we would all learn. Not only would it expand our knowledge but our horizons and concepts as well. Patients can only benefit.

Kelly Turner (best-selling author of 'Radical Remission: Surviving Cancer Against All Odds') tracked and documented patients who had made remarkable recoveries from very serious conditions, writing a PhD thesis on that. She continues her work. Healing is possible.

Recently I heard from an 85-year-old client who reported that, after a few months of treatment, she had more energy than she had had for over 50 years. Her hands had been so arthritic that almost no movement was possible in her right hand. Now, she is opening and closing her hand easily and virtually full dexterity has returned.

It is understandable but regrettable that so many medical professionals are hamstrung, having to follow the protocols of treatment as set down by the National Institute for Clinical Excellence (NICE). Doctors can be sued for not following the protocols of this committee. I remember a doctor saying that she couldn't recommend beetroot juice or cayenne pepper to someone with arterial disease because it wasn't approved, yet statins are, so that's what she had to prescribe.

There is, without question, a great need for pharmaceuticals and scalpels, of course there is and there always will be, yet surely they must be applied as a last resort not as a first requirement. In my experience, there is a lot that can be done before their involvement is inevitable. Many other techniques are gentle, simple and not invasive. They are certainly cheaper. In my view the public deserves access to all other available modalities of treatment so that their whole health can improve and they can engage wholeheartedly in the process of healing, rather than being passive recipients of prescribed treatments.

Having shaken off the shackles of working within such a constrained system, I have continued to expand my treatment options, continually learning techniques that filled gaps in my knowledge and effectiveness. Subsequent to completing my medical degree, I have had training and experience in:

- Osteopathy
- Acupuncture/Laser Acupuncture
- Auricular Medicine
- Nutrition
- Homeopathy
- Autonomic Resonance Testing
- Electronic Gem Therapy
- Neuro Electric Therapy

- Kinetic Chain Release
- Thought Field Therapy
- BICOM
- Gamma Mindset
- Journey work
- Non-Linear Scanning
- Frequency Specific Microcurrent

The beauty of many of these techniques is that they are endlessly informative; the body tells you what the issues are if you are trained, aware and receptive.

The approaches I have chosen to invest in are those that give me insight beyond the physical level into the emotional and mental levels. As I have already alluded to, I have found that it is only when changes occur on these deeper levels that physical healing can happen and become permanent. I have therefore not prescribed any pharmaceuticals in the last 25 years with only one exception.

Incidentally most of this learning was not considered as legitimate Continuing Professional Development (CPD) by the General Medical Council. Latterly they contacted me to question whether my professional learning met their approved standards. The 'official' CPD offered over the years was largely focused on more conventional subjects, which I felt disinclined to attend.

The General Medical Council have the power to withhold a doctor's licence to practise unless they keep developing their learning along what I see as a very blinkered route. Although of course I can appreciate the need for maintaining standards, codes of conduct and continual learning, seeing the conceptual myopia of the General Medical Council led me to voluntarily erase my membership. They are a watchdog meant to protect the public. From my perspective they are constraining and confining what doctors do, sometimes to their detriment. Nil else beyond the NICE guidelines is deemed acceptable, regardless of how useful or successful other approaches might be. Incidentally, several of my clients have passed on my name to their consultants, commenting that 'you could probably learn something from this man's approach'. But to this day, I have yet to receive any communication from an NHS doctor or consultant who was eager to understand more about what I was doing, and seek a partnered approach.

Having stated my fundamental beliefs, I reserve that wonderful, fundamental human right to be wrong, which forever keeps me humble. I continue to learn so much from that.

TOXINS: THE ROOT OF ALL DISEASE

To begin to understand the impact of toxins and their fundamental role in driving the development of illness, I'll share a simple analogy. Typically, we trust a driver to be safely in command of a car. However, when the driver has been drinking alcohol, they may still be in command of the car yet their functioning is compromised: reaction time is slower, perceptions of distance and speed distorted and it can end very messily, sometimes fatally.

Clearly, the difference between the safe driver and the drunk driver is intoxication.

The command mechanisms in a cell are very similar. When the nutrient and information flows are pure and normal, the cell sparkles with healthy function. Unsurprisingly, toxin exposure compromises cell function. Although cells have normal detoxing mechanisms, when the limitations of these detoxing systems have been exceeded, the level of compromise becomes permanent. Cell function then becomes messy; the cell may even die yet the replacement cells face the same toxicity, so continuing the compromise. Illness then results, or even whole system death. The cells or systems are drunk with toxins.

In its broadest sense, a toxin is anything that interferes with the flow of energy to cells, tissues, organs and systems in the body. Therefore, toxins disrupt normal healthy cell function, leading to changes in the physiology and biochemistry of those cells and their associated systems.

In a healthy system, the body's innate detoxing mechanisms act to neutralise any toxins and so allow normal healthy function to continue. In illness, the body's detoxing mechanisms are overwhelmed by the toxic load. In other words, illness and disease are caused by the body's inability to withstand the impact of a combination of toxins.

Toxins are commonly thought of as chemical poisons, sitting on a scientist's shelf with an ominous skull and crossbones symbol on the label. However, in reality, they can be much more commonplace, coming from both the internal and the external environment, and they can be physical, emotional or mental in origin.

The most common sources are:

PHYSICAL

- Food intolerance / poor diet
- Chemical toxins (weed-killers, pesticides, insecticides, pharmaceutical residues)
- Environmental pollution (geopathic stress and 'techno-smog' ie electromagnetic radiation)
- Heavy metals (eg mercury from amalgam fillings or vaccine residues)
- Air pollution
- Microbes (viruses, bacteria, fungi)

MENTAL

- Habitual negative thinking / worry
- Habitual negative judgement / attitude
- Mental overwhelm / stress

EMOTIONAL

- Unexpressed emotions
- Unresolved emotional issues
- Trauma

FOOD INTOLERANCE

When I began to look at whole health and not just localised symptoms, I was astonished by the number of people I saw who had food intolerance as a major contributor to their symptom complex. It was never mentioned as even a possible component of disease development in my student days, except with gluten intolerance in Coeliac disease. Yet I now view nutrition as one of the primary foundations of health, and will spend time exploring it with every client.

Also, having seen the immense impact that diet can have, I have become more and more passionate about it (much to the irritation of those who hear me talk about it over and over again!). I just can't stress enough how important it is. Often people don't believe it until they really give it a go, and stick to their dietary exclusions 100%.

I recall one client who came to see me only once. He had chronic indigestion and had been diagnosed as having a hiatus hernia. After identifying his intolerances, his immediate reaction to my suggestions left me unsure as to what his level of commitment was about his food regime. I didn't hear from him again. A few weeks later, another client arrived who knew this man. She said he was recommending my services to anyone who would listen because all his symptoms had gone completely and he was off all medication.

Digestive conditions are the most obvious casualty of food intolerance, yet I have found that all of the following illnesses have food intolerance as a cardinal contributor:

Acne (pustular), anxiety and depression, arterial disease, arthritis, asthma, bedwetting, constipation, Crohn's disease, croup, diabetes, diarrhoea, dry skin, duodenal ulcer, eczema, heart-burn, hiatus hernia, hypertension, irritable bowel syndrome (IBS), indigestion, lack of energy, migraine, obesity, paranoia, recurrent sinusitis, recurrent sore throat and tonsillitis, schizophrenia, ulcerative colitis, vertigo.

If you suspect that some element of diet is negatively impacting your health, it is always advisable to get individually tested for your own intolerances. Having tested thousands of people, my findings are that the following foods are most commonly *not* tolerated:

- Dairy products (eggs are often OK); here 'dairy' means milk, butter, cream, cheese, ice cream, kefir, yoghurt, whey, it often needs to include beef as well.
- Caffeine
- Sugar
- Wheat / gluten

Surprisingly, I have also discovered that the effect of eating the rogue foods is *not* dose related. Any amount of the offending food is toxic or, to put it another way, a teaspoonful is as bad as a ton.

For some, a change of diet can be a huge undertaking, especially when it includes several ubiquitous foods, but the effects make it worth the effort. Clients have told me over the years that the benefits of sticking absolutely to a new nutritional regime, and eating <u>utterly none</u> of the prohibited foods, include:

- more energy, stamina and exercise tolerance
- better quality sleep
- no need to snack
- appetite is much more normal
- weight loss – typically losing about 1lb a week without effort. (Menstruating women typically lose 3lb per month, and nothing in the premenstrual week)
- clear head and better concentration
- much more even temperament, much less volatile, no depression, no anxiety

- increased libido
- the need for medication is much reduced, often leading to needing no medication at all
- a change of attitude – even the thought of the toxic food can seem unappealing

It's worth flagging up a warning here that soon after starting a new diet regime, the symptoms relating to the toxic foods usually get markedly worse before they disappear. Eczema typically becomes spectacular for a while, and then fades to disappearance, usually within 14 to 21 days. People with Arthritis, especially those with Rheumatoid and particularly those with Ankylosing Spondylitis, have much increased symptoms which can last three to four months during the detox phase.

Some people also go through a phase where they become exquisitely sensitive to even tiny amounts of the toxic foods. Also, after detoxing, people may become acutely aware when they have (even innocently) eaten something that they are intolerant to because some of their previous symptoms quickly spark up.

A curiosity: When I was 8 to 10 years old, I seemed to have no problem with milk, butter, bread or cheese. I don't know what has happened to those foods since then: has their processing changed? Or is it me – have I changed? I have zero tolerance to these products now.

Another curiosity: when I started testing for food intolerance in 1982 the vast majority were reacting adversely to dairy products, as well as to coffee, chocolate, cocoa and cola. I rarely found wheat intolerance. At a guess I might find 100 people with milk intolerance for every 1 with an adverse reaction to wheat. Now it is pretty much even, as many being intolerant to wheat as are to milk.

I wonder why this is. What has changed? Has widespread use of glyphosate (a common weed-killer) changed the wheat into an unacceptable form? If so, does it make other inorganic cereals metabolically unacceptable too?

Another consequence of having focused in depth on the effects of food is that I now know with absolute certainty that there is a profound link between diet and behaviour. Those who have prominent psychiatric symptoms seem to have utter disbelief in the notion that foods have any impact on their mental state. I have observed such changes in temperament in every one when they change their nutrition to embrace only that to which the body is tolerant.

GUT, HEART, BRAIN: THE CONNECTIONS

Definitions:

Microbiome – The population of gazillions of healthy bacteria in the body (mostly in the gut).

Dysbiosis – The presence of unhealthy bacteria in both number and type, which contributes to illness.

Gut – The entire digestive tract running from mouth to anus.

The longest nerve in the body is the Vagus nerve, running from brainstem to part of the colon. It influences the heart, lungs and digestive tract. The direction of flow of information in the Vagus nerve is 10% from brainstem to colon, and 90% from colon to heart, lungs and brain.

Therefore gut health can influence the proper functioning of the heart, (e.g. funny rhythms), lungs in terms of a wheeze for example, (so explaining a mechanism behind dairy intolerance and Asthma), and brain, in terms of anxiety and depression and other psychiatric conditions. Other mental health implications include poor concentration, mind filled with cotton wool, and poor educational performance. Thus a myriad of illnesses may originate in the dysbiosis in the gut, and unless the microbiome is restored to health then the downstream effects of the dysbiosis can only recur and continue.

Keeping a healthy microbiome, through a healthy diet and probiotic supplements where needed, is vital for maintaining good health. A probiotic is a mixture of bugs that live happily in the intestines and which restore healthy function to the gut microbiome. The probiotic I take, has 12 types of happy bug in it. I also take barley grass at the same time to keep my system alkaline.

Everyone I have seen who had a food intolerance and dysbiosis has remarked on major improvements in their temperament when these issues have been addressed.

Rachel came to see me after having over 10 years of debilitating anxiety and depression. Despite having received various treatments on the NHS and taking the prescribed medication, little was making a difference and her quality of life was significantly compromised. After her first visit, and after implementing her new dietary changes, Rachel was able to come off her medication. After the second visit, she continued to have more energy and more mental clarity and was able to re-establish her own business. Her symptoms disappeared completely and at the time of re-establishing contact (six years after the consultation), she was still feeling well. (Her story is featured in the *'In Their Own Write'* chapter).

If this is of interest to you, a couple of recommended resources are 'The Broken Brain' mini-series by Dr Mark Hyman (www.brokenbrain.com) and the book *Feed My Brain: Eating to Excel* by Schauss, AG, Friedlander, B and Meyer, A. Another book that precedes these by decades is 'Not All in the Mind' by Dr. Richard Mackarness.

I'm sure it was Schauss who advised a prison in the US to change the nutrition of a psychopath in their care, with particular regard to his intake of refined sugar. This guy was usually in solitary confinement. When he came out, he would be violent towards other prisoners within a short time and have to go back into solitary. This was an endless pattern. If my memory serves, it took the prisoner 22 months of zero refined sugar and other dietary changes after which he was a calm, delightful pussycat of a man.

In how many prisons would you find sugar on every meal table? How many others in society need their nutrition changed to see massive changes in temperament?

I wonder to what extent psychiatrists and psychologists explore this. Of course, the impact of trauma and other adverse life events needs to be addressed but to what extent is the brain being banjaxed by bizarre metabolism from inappropriate nutrition?

How valuable is it to talk to someone who is drunk when trying to change their behaviour? It makes much more sense to get them detoxed and sober then offer the counselling because now they are receptive. Isn't it the same for all psychiatric conditions? Surely when someone is detoxed the therapies have much greater likelihood of success.

THE QUALITY OF WHAT WE EAT

It is not just the kind of food that we need to consider, the quality also has a significant bearing on our health.

How many pesticides, herbicides, fungicides have been used on it? And what kind were they? What kind of fertiliser was used? What was in the water that was sprayed on it?

Farmers now spray their non-organic cereal crops with glyphosate, typically two weeks before harvest. Glyphosate has been characterised as a probable carcinogen by the World Health Organisation. Its use plumps up the seeds and dries them in some way, in a process they call 'desiccation'. This gives the farmer a bigger yield by weight and means there's less need to dry the crop once it is harvested and so results in more money.

What happens to that glyphosate? It is absorbed into the grain. The grain is ground into flour to make bread, cakes, biscuits, and it is an additive in so many foods such as sausages. Evidently, all of these foods then come to contain glyphosate and it becomes established in the food chain. I find that glyphosate is an insidious contributor to many illnesses in the people I see.

Barley is treated similarly and the glyphosate therefore becomes part of the beer or lager that results from fermentation. Rice also has glyphosate in it, unless it is truly organic. The run-off from the farmers' fields will also contain glyphosate, which flows into the streams and rivers and oceans to return in rainfall.

My advice – eat Organic when you can.

NUTRITIONAL DEFICIENCIES

Many people believe they are eating healthily yet they have a relative deficiency, meaning that the demands of their individual metabolic state need more than they are ingesting or absorbing.

I test every client for deficiencies in vitamins, minerals, omega oils and so on, and let them know how to remedy this.

Nutrient deficiency arises from the depletion of the soil by intensive farming, therefore even 'healthy' foods may provide insufficient vitamins and minerals. Eating organically goes some way towards avoiding that. Getting tested for these deficiencies at least annually puts minds at rest and metabolism at peace.

This is a substantial topic and I can only scratch the surface here, but these are my most common findings: The most frequent need in all cases, especially where there is a strong psychiatric component, and in everyone with cancer or leukaemia, is for more Vitamin D3. I find that most clients with these conditions need 10,000 units (250 micrograms) of D3 daily for anything up to 4 months, occasionally longer. For healthier clients I often suggest 5,000 units (125 micrograms) daily throughout autumn, winter and early spring, stopping for the sunny summer months and resuming in autumn.

I have also found that correcting the microbiome with probiotics and alkalising supplements is essential in almost all cases. This helps make nutritional absorption become more effective.

People suffering from stress and depression may well benefit from taking Ubiquinol and Acetyl-L-Carnitine to boost the function in the exhausted mitochondria. The more elderly the client the more likelihood that they will need Ubiquinol to boost the energy production within the mitochondria – the tiny energy factories in the cells.

In August 2020 I have only just become aware of Iodine deficiency as a possible major contributor to a whole range of illnesses. The book 'The Iodine Crisis' by Lynne Farrow is my first source of this information.

How you Cook

Do you use a Microwave oven?

It is not so much the heating effect of the microwaves that is important; it is that specific microwave frequencies change the form of the amino acids in a way that makes them indigestible.

Let me explain just a little of the chemistry. Proteins are chains of amino acids, and amino acids have shapes-in-space called an L-form and a D-form. They are what is named 'Isomers'. This means that their shapes are mirror-images of each other, in exactly the same way that your right and left hands are mirror images and not identical.

The body is designed to metabolise the L-forms of amino acids, but not the D-forms. As the process of microwaving converts amino acids from the L-form to the D-form, this means that the body can't handle them and any nutrients in the microwaved food cannot be assimilated.

GEOPATHIC STRESS

Moving away from the topic of food, but still in the arena of physical toxins is Geopathic Stress. Evidently, human beings are an integral part of the wider eco-system and therefore we are continually impacted by our environment. Although we have clearly adapted to live successfully with some environmental discomfort, our health can, without question, be negatively impacted by the energy in our environment. The term 'Geopathic Stress' refers to the energy of an environment, which is supporting illness not health.

Whether Geopathic Stress comes from natural or man-made sources, it is usually invisible and therefore easy to dismiss. However, the impact can be significant. Something about the energies in the place is impeding normal healthy metabolism.

In alignment with the generic title, the stress may be geological, such as the presence of underground streams or fault lines, or it could be technological, from WiFi, phone masts and other sources of Electro Magnetic Forces [EMF]. These have come increasingly to the fore in the last 20 years. There seems to be a great degree of individual sensitivity to these forces as their presence in our environment expands exponentially.

I just don't understand the widespread blindness to the effects of EMFs on humans, animals, vegetation, birds and insects, and the extraordinary amount that they contribute to disease. Increasingly I read about cancers and strokes in 20-year-olds, and every case of Leukaemia or brain tumour I have seen has EMFs as a major factor in their development. I strongly believe that cell phone towers are not innocent and safe, neither are mobile phones. The presence of 2.45 GHz in 5G radiation means that amino acids, and therefore proteins, will be under continual push to change from the healthy L-form to the incompatible D-form (as described in the section on microwaving food). Similarly, my finding is that 'leaky gut' is associated with regular, continuous exposure to EMFs.

It is the responsibility of the providers of these radiations and devices to *prove* that they are safe, *before* they are inflicted on a gullible public; rather than to announce them as exciting developments and push that with massive propaganda.

[The British Society of Dowsers has many experts who can detect and correct these toxic vibes. In the USA certified Building Biologists have equivalent skills].

The most susceptible area of the house is the bedroom. This is important because you are in bed for nearly one-third of each day, thus your exposure to any Geopathic Stress that is present is recurrent and constant. Infants often instinctively move away from this kind of stress, which may be one explanation as to why they can be found at the other end of their cot in the morning! Professionals in this field also believe that cats are attracted to places with Geopathic Stress, whereas dogs hate it. If the cat likes to sleep on your bed, it may not just be for the warmth and comfort; it is highly likely that this stress is affecting your bedroom, ultimately draining your health and increasing the likelihood of developing illnesses (particularly cancers, brain tumours and leukaemias).

Unfortunately, there are fewer and fewer places free from EMFs so I suspect this does not bode well for the health of those people who are particularly sensitive to them. Recommendations to minimise Geopathic Stress and techno-vibes:

- Give your DECT (Digital Enhanced Cordless Telecommunications) phone to the dustbin. These are the ones that sit on a base station, but you can take them anywhere. Why? Because they fill the house with microwaves 24/7, regardless of whether you are using it or not.
- Switch off Wi-Fi at night. It adds microwaves to the microwave soup from the DECT phones.
- Do not charge your mobile phone at the bedside. The electromagnetic field is too close to your head for too long. Mobile phones work by receiving and transmitting microwaves.
- Always use wired headphones (not Bluetooth) when talking on your cell phone, and keep the phone as far away from your body as possible e.g. on a table in front of you.
- If you have to have your phone at your bedside, ensure it is in aeroplane mode overnight.
- When you are moving around, keep your phone in aeroplane mode or put it in a bag rather than in a pocket or a bra. NB Ladies who put their mobile phone in their bra usually developed a cancer in that breast; if you have it in your trouser pocket then testicles, prostate, ovaries, cervix, intestines, bones, muscles are continuously exposed to the microwaves. This can lead to infertility as well as cancers.

In summary, all physical toxins will upset the body's metabolism in some way, and their effects extend way beyond the physical body. Therefore, even if an illness appears to be in the mental or emotional domains, ignoring the physical elements would be, in my view, a major omission.

Evidently, there is a huge amount of information freely available on the myriad of physical toxins – dietary, technological, chemical and environmental. My aim here is just to give a flavour of the ones I've had most experience of and which I believe are most central to illness.

MENTAL AND EMOTIONAL TOXINS

Despite the undeniable effect of physical toxins, what I've come to believe is that almost all illness acquired through life begins on the mental and emotional level, with an unresolved issue.

Given how fundamental I believe this to be, allow me to reiterate what I already explained in the section 'Beyond Convention 1' on the body as an energetic system: at the outset, the initial root cause issue was simply an event that happened. This event, whatever it was, is an objective fact. Facts do not have emotions or feelings. However, in line with the typical human habit, whoever is involved makes a judgement about what happened. And, in turn, these judgements spark an emotional reaction.

The emotions that arise are either expressed and discharged at the time, or they remain within the body. When these emotions are not expressed (especially the negative ones) they continue to fester. In the immediate aftermath, the event is often replayed over and over in the mind, reinforcing the negative energies with each reminder.

Longer term, without adequate expression, these emotions become completely suppressed. They leave the conscious mind and become held in the subconscious where, alongside associated limiting beliefs, they continue to influence behaviour without our awareness.

The continued disturbance created by the unexpressed emotions makes the body vulnerable to the effects of additional toxins. In fact, intense negative emotion held in check for long periods can wreak havoc in the body, giving rise to a whole host of uncomfortable symptoms. This susceptibility increases with time, producing an accelerating downward spiral towards a more embedded illness.

EMOTIONS AND ILLNESS

In the 1990s, when I realised that all illness begins on the mental and emotional levels, I thought I had discovered something new. That was until I opened my textbook on Chinese acupuncture: there I read the statement that an excess of core emotions is the cause of all endogenous disease.

"It is that the *excess* of emotions such as Anger, Melancholy, Grief, Fear, Fright are the source of all endogenous disease." *(Essentials of Chinese Acupuncture, published by Foreign Languages Press, Beijing, China; page 44).*

Even though the link between suppressed unresolved emotions and organs has been known for many millennia in Chinese medicine, it has not been acknowledged in the West until the early part of the 20th century.

Personally, I acknowledged that I was a few thousand years behind the curve, but at least I felt confirmed in my findings.

My own research and practice over 30+ years has revealed the following correlations between suppressed emotions and their impact on the organs and systems in the body:

- Lungs associated with grief
- Liver, with anger
- Bladder, with hurt feelings, being pissed off
- Gallbladder, with guilt, resentment
- Kidney, with fear, dogma
- Heart, with heartache, lack of joy
- Prostate/Uterus, with loneliness
- Spleen and Pancreas with all the above

Even though fear is primarily associated with the kidneys, when it is unresolved and suppressed, this affects ALL systems and organs in the body. Similarly, anger affects most systems in the body. Consequently, unexpressed anger may contribute to the onset of joint problems, muscle pain, fibromyalgia, lowered immunity, heart problems and no doubt several others. Surely, it would be easier to deal with the anger than with the vast range of possible resulting symptoms.

All the unresolved and suppressed energies are bound in cells, tissues and organs. Their continued presence acts as toxins affecting those structures. I find that the pancreas and spleen seem to be a sponge for all suppressed emotions.

It would therefore seem essential that suppressed emotional energies are dealt with, otherwise recurrence or persistence of the illness or disease condition is inevitable. Thus dealing solely with the physical expressions of illness or disease can never be 100% successful in the long term.

As Candace Pert states in 'Molecules of Emotion' - "*I am of the strong opinion that complementary therapies can not only help with chronic degenerative diseases... but also with other health problems... for which conventional medicine can offer only incomplete or no help.*"

LONG-TERM EFFECTS – AN ILLUSTRATION

Suppressed anger is held mostly in the liver, with some residues also retained within the spleen and pancreas. The liver is responsible for storing and regulating the flow of blood, and the external organ connected with the liver is the eye.

Jack (in his 50s) came to see me with a disturbance in his field of vision. His ophthalmic specialist had discovered that the blood supply to his optic nerve was partially compromised. During our consultation, testing revealed that Jack had experienced an event, age 5, that had resulted in a significant level of anger. I call this the 'seed' event (which most typically happens between age 5-10).

At the time of the consultation, nothing immediately came to mind, as it had long ago been forgotten. However, as a consequence of the probing, a deeply upsetting memory arose from Jack's subconscious. He recalled his first day at school, shortly after he had been dropped off. Alone in the playground, he looked round to see the reassuring faces of his parents, only to find that they had gone. The sudden realisation of their perceived abandonment brought instant panic and he screamed. For some time, he was inconsolable such was the depth of his distress.

Jack was able to revisit this event from a mature adult perspective and work through the unresolved emotion. Soon after the emotional resolution, his eyesight began to improve.

EMOTIONS AND BUGS

Throughout medical school and my conventional professional life I was taught about the importance of bacteria, fungi, viruses, parasites (colloquially termed 'bugs'), and their contribution to illness and disease. This way of looking at illness is most commonly known as 'Germ Theory', which presumes that certain diseases are caused by the invasion of the body by microorganisms.

In alignment with my approach re focusing on causes, when I carry out testing on people, not only do I look for which bugs are active on the physical level but I also identify the emotions present.

When the emotions are detected, I also test their intensity, and am able to put these into an order which shows which one is the most powerful, which one is the second most powerful and so on. This allows me to deduce which bugs and which emotions are having the greatest impact on the client's condition.

One day in 2004 I got a 'nudge' to try something more. I got the intuitive prod to check the second most powerful emotion against the dominant bug and go through the microbes again; then the third most powerful against the bug, go through the microbes once more and see what came up. Little did I know it, but what I was about to do changed my view of Bacteriology for ever.

Essentially what I discovered was that the bug was very likely to change depending on which emotion was dominant. In other words, when the internal environment (i.e. the terrain) changed – first energetically, then biochemically – it would stimulate the bug to mutate into something different. I guess when you think about it, it's simple chemistry. The main difference being that the energetic shift happens first as it always does. You may recall me saying that energetic change happens via photons, which move at the speed of light, whereas chemical molecules have some mass and therefore inertia and take longer to change.

Let me give a couple of examples from real people.

One man I saw had the Rotavirus as his main bug. On testing I found he also had a complex mix of emotions. Following the process outlined above, I looked at what would happen to the Rotavirus in the presence of the different suppressed emotions.

What I found was that the combined effect of Rotavirus with six different emotions, resulted in energetic frequencies equivalent to four different bugs. One of these bugs was the Herpes virus, and interestingly he went on to develop Shingles (also called Herpes Zoster) between the first and second consultation.

Within a few weeks of treatment, another of those four highlighted bugs (Prion) did not come up in testing, indicating that we had dealt adequately with the underlying emotion.

In another client with the same dominant bug (Rotavirus) but a very different complex of suppressed emotions, the expression over time was markedly different. The table below gives an indication of how each emotion was contributing to a different expression of illness.

With this Suppressed Emotion	Rotavirus mutated to	Client's expression
Terror	Pertussis (whooping cough)	Had this twice as a child
Lack of interest/withdrawal/ self-repression	Fungi	Actively present and recurrent
Extreme anguish	Rubella	Had as a child
Anger / resentment	Ostitis	Went on to develop a dental abscess
Hopelessness	Prion	Associated with Dementia

In short, every condition that was indicated as a likely consequence of her underlying emotions, had been experienced by this client, with the exception of Prion. Given that Prion is associated with Dementia, dealing with the associated emotion (Hopelessness in this case) may in theory help to prevent the future onset of Dementia, though I will never know in this case.

In the case of one fascinating lady, the dominant bug, Chickenpox, combined with six different emotions produced frequencies equivalent to only two different bugs, one of which was Prion. When I reviewed her notes 10 years later and contacted the family, I discovered she had been admitted to a home for long-term care just two days before my phone call. She had Dementia. I still wonder whether this imprint could have been reversed if I had been able to see her more often over a longer period and shift the emotional burden.

I have tested hundreds of clients in this way and eventually reached the conclusion that there was no point in worrying about the presenting bug. If the emotional terrain could be changed, the bug would change. Put another way, our underlying emotions determine which bug is expressed in our body and which illness develops.

Now, in this context, I only concern myself with the underlying emotions. Incidentally, this is also why I don't actively advocate vaccinations, instead helping clients change their terrain so it is inhospitable to infectious disease.

STRESS AND THE PRESSURE COOKER SYNDROME

Everyone experiences challenging events in their lives and is consequently exposed to many of the toxins I've described – physical, mental and emotional. Unquestionably these toxins create major stress, yet the body has an extraordinary level of resilience to withstand them. However, as the natural resilience is slowly eroded so the body becomes more susceptible to the effect of various toxins. In this way, food intolerances, Geopathic Stress, heavy metals, microbes, EMFs etc, often become more actively toxic because the body can no longer hold them in check. Therefore, a downward spiral is sparked as cell metabolism and organ function become increasingly compromised as each toxin enters the arena.

What has struck me as a pattern is what I call the 'Pressure Cooker Syndrome'.

During a period of major stress, such as caring for a loved one who is very ill, the individual copes valiantly with whatever immediate challenges they face. They may be sleep-deprived, have had irregular, inadequate meals and feel as if they have been run ragged, yet somehow they are still on their feet and are still managing to cope – just.

However, there is a cost. The body has run on adrenaline and cortisol, no sleep, little nutrition while dealing with the emergency. Once the emergency is over, the adrenaline is still pouring until the realisation is made that the recent helter-skelter of activity can now come to a close.

Now the body needs to recover. In fact, it is not just the body; it is the whole Being that needs care, sustenance, peace and rest. What happens next, how long it takes and what the outcome is depends very much on the nature and duration of the original major stressful event.

If grief arises as a result of this event, especially if this involves the death of very close relative, the recovery will be slow and over the long term.

The impact of the death of a loved one often precedes a heart attack some 18 months later in the surviving partner. If they wish to join their departed, or have no real wish to continue living, then they too will probably die from such an event.

On coming out of the Pressure Cooker, they get colds, flu, gastric bugs, migraines, it might even be the initial stimulus for the generation of cancer or leukaemia in years to come. Everything that the body has suppressed throughout the duration of the crisis now has expression.

This is the Pressure Cooker Syndrome – coping in a crisis and crashing afterwards.

SUMMARY OF FACTORS IMPACTING HEALTH

The diagram gives an overview of the multiple factors impacting on our health and energy, all of which need to be addressed if full healing is to happen.

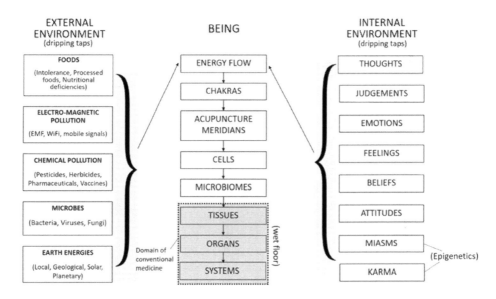

UNCOVERING TOXINS – WHERE THE MAGIC BEGINS

Given the extensive range of toxins that are possible contributors, time is a crucial component in getting to the root of illness. The other critical factor is having the ability to uncover them. This is where the magic really begins, and where I imagine my 'Witch Doctor' eponym comes from. The term 'magic' is used when people can't see or don't understand how something happened. Without this understanding, they think I have magical powers. Here are a couple of examples to illustrate:

THE DISBELIEVING HOUSEWIFE

Sadie came to see me with a persistent cough. All treatments and investigations she had tried thus far had generated no benefit.

I tested her and consequently told her that she had fungal spores in her house, which must be damp somewhere. She looked at me incredulously and said:

"That's impossible. My house is brand-new and I've only been living in it for six weeks."

When she stormed out her body language, her demeanour and her curt language indicated to me that she thought she had wasted her time and money and that I was a charlatan.

Twenty years later I was at a birthday party and happened to be sitting next to a woman, Carol, who knew Sadie. Carol asked,

"Did Sadie ever contact you again?" "No" I replied, after which Carol told me the following story.

A few weeks after seeing me, Sadie went into her bathroom and noticed something curious where the shower tray met the floor. The builder was still building more houses along the same road so she went along to see him to discuss her concern. He duly came to the house and pulled up part of the bathroom floor to investigate. They were met by the sight of a forest of fungi. A cold-water supply pipe had not been properly connected and had been dripping constantly. All the necessary repairs were then carried out. Subsequently her cough stopped. Carol urged Sadie to contact me and tell me what had happened, yet that didn't happen. I can only imagine she was a little embarrassed by the extent of her initial disgruntlement.

THE BEMUSED ELECTRICIAN

During one consultation I found that my client Sheena was exposed to Electro Stress. I picked up the possibility that there was some fault in her electrical supply or wiring, which was having a toxic effect on her. I further deduced that the problem might well lie with the earth wire.

On that basis Sheena called an electrician to come and visit and check her circuitry. He duly took up a floorboard in her hallway and investigated the earth wire. To his surprise he found that this wire was the wrong calibre and, even more alarmingly, was not connected to anything; it just stopped part way under the hall floor.

He asked Sheena if another electrician had tested her system and found a problem. She replied: "No, a Doctor had suggested it."

She said that his expression was priceless.

The magic in detecting this is certainly not just in me. I did say at the start of the book that I have learned techniques which enable me to tap into the extraordinary wisdom and history of the body. Yet, in this case (and every other one for that matter), there is no way I could have picked up that issue unless it was stored in the client's body.

I've mentioned the word 'testing' a number of times and not really given much detail, so let me do my best to uncover a little bit of the science behind the magic.

Biofeedback is the generic name for any testing that gathers information from the body. There are plenty of common technological devices that do this, from a simple blood pressure monitor to highly sophisticated scanners.

What I work with is natural biofeedback. What I mean by this is that the body instinctively reacts to certain stimuli.

Some of these reactions are obvious and others are very subtle. An example of an obvious reaction would be if a person was phobic to spiders. If I started to talk about spiders or pointed out that there was one crawling along the ceiling, I would be able to see the person's pupils dilating, their muscles tensing, their breathing pattern change etc. What is fascinating, and key to me doing what I do, is that if that same person was sitting in front of me and I started merely thinking about spiders, some part of their consciousness would pick this up and would respond in a subtle, but detectable, way.

Based on this principle, the Vega-testing system that I use, is able to detect people's subtle responses to the questions I pose. As I mentioned in the introduction, I ask these questions silently (i.e. I just 'think' the question) and I can measure a response in the client. Their responses are picked up with a highly sensitive electrical probe that is applied to an acupuncture point on one of their fingers.

I accept that this may sound far-fetched but I've been doing it for nearly 40 years and I have come to trust it implicitly. Most clients are gobsmacked by what can be found using this method and without it, I would never be able to achieve the results I do.

Going back to the NHS for a moment, I now see that doctors have an impossible task if they hope to uncover anything as useful for their patients in an appointment time of 7-10 minutes. How much meaningful progress can be made when there is a need to investigate, understand and undo potentially decades of disease development?

In my experience (and that of many, many people who have come to see me), healing is always much more rapid and long-lasting when you can truly understand the whole spectrum of causal factors.

HEALING: RETURNING THE BODY TO ITS DEFAULT SETTING

In the right conditions, our bodies have an innate capability to find their own way back to health. Healing is the body's default setting.

Nature is amazing to provide us with such an extraordinary and intelligent self-healing system. All we as physicians and therapists need to do is to help the patient create an environment in which the natural processes can work their inherent magic. I always believe that this can be done, even in the most challenging of circumstances. With that in mind, if a body has produced a disease then I believe my role as a doctor is to stimulate the being to *un*-produce it.

However, toxic tissue cannot heal; only cleansed tissue can. Full healing only happens when all toxins of every type have been eradicated. This means that healing has to happen on all levels (Physical, Emotional, Mental and Spiritual) before someone can be proclaimed 'cured'.

There is a common assumption that a cure has been achieved when the physical level is restored to full function. Once a person feels better physically, understandably they feel relieved and may assume their healing is complete. Typically, they then go back to normal life and are mega dismayed and surprised when recurrence happens some weeks, months or even years later. This common pattern simply indicates that focusing purely on the physical is an incomplete approach; the other, deeper levels need attention too. Changing from a diseased pattern of energies to a healthy pattern, particularly in chronic conditions is always a long-term challenge.

I have already mentioned Dr Kelly Turner who published a book, called 'Radical Remission' in 2014 after researching many cancer patients who had made full recoveries, often against the odds. Included in the nine fundamental factors that emerged as vital to the healing process, was the need to eliminate toxins on each of the levels:

- Physical – diet and supplements
- Mental – having a strong reason for living
- Emotional – releasing suppressed emotions and increasing positive emotions
- Spiritual – Deepening your spiritual connection

I find it immensely reassuring that recoveries previously considered as 'miraculous' are now better understood. That way, we need no longer feel passive and powerless with the belief that our health is dependent on a distant, unseen force, but that it is very much in our own hands.

That said, just to be annoyingly paradoxical, I also believe that karma has a part to play. What this means from a personal perspective is that I do everything I can to support my own health, and that of others, then I let go. I keep going as far as I possibly can, until I can do nothing more but accept whatever outcome unfolds.

DETOXING

Detoxing is the name given to the process of getting toxins out of the body. Healing simply cannot happen without it. Detoxing serves to remove the obstacles to normal energy flow in the body (much like releasing a log-jam in a river) so that tissues can be restored to health.

Once detoxing has started there is no point in re-toxing the body with what you are trying to get rid of – clearly this just prolongs the process.

Once the source and identity of the toxins has been determined, whether these are from the internal environment (e.g. negative beliefs, emotions, chemical residues) or from the external environment (pollutants, food, electromagnetic fields [EMFs] etc), the patient can begin to eliminate their exposure. The easiest thing to start with is to neutralise the external toxins completely, otherwise they become a continuing source of pathological energy. Therefore, as much as possible, clean air, water and food needs to be consumed, and food exclusions rigidly adhered to. Also, as I mentioned earlier minimising exposure to EMFs can be a critical component.

Once the detox begins, something paradoxical happens: the patient starts to feel worse. This is fairly typical and is an important part of the healing reaction.

During the detox process, the toxins leave their hidey-holes in the cells and tissues and migrate into the blood stream, so the amount of circulating toxins increases, thus the symptoms associated with these toxins return and become emphasised.

Although leaving the client feeling terrible, it is actually very encouraging; it shows that the approach is working. In particular illnesses, some clients have a really torrid time with a dramatic worsening of their symptoms. This worsening can last up to three or four months in some, especially with Rheumatoid Arthritis, to the point where they can't bear the increase in joint pain, and its intransigence, any longer. They then resume their old habits and so the possibility of them getting rid of the Rheumatoid diminishes.

Those with Ankylosing Spondylitis (a type of arthritis in the spine) can go through the same thing. The older the client, the longer the healing reaction; in an 85 year old it took a year. (See Osteoarthrosis in part 3)

The circulating toxins pass through the liver and on to exit via the bowels. This may cause temporary diarrhoea or constipation and, as the toxins go through the kidneys they exit via the urine, which may sting or smell or be of greater volume than usual. Any apparent cystitis is just that: apparent; there is no need for antibiotics. Other means of eliminating toxins are via lungs, sinuses or skin. A cough, wheeze, runny nose, sinusitis or skin rashes may develop; yet they are all temporary. In menstruating women, their periods provide another means of exit from the body; indeed, their first period after beginning the detox is often much heavier than usual, illustrating that detoxification is happening.

The detoxing process can be assisted by drinking a lot more water. If you have access to a steam room or sauna (including Infra-Red), that too will aid the cleansing.

The duration of this detoxing stage is highly individual and therefore unpredictable though, in general, the younger the patient the shorter the detox time.

The most unfortunate detox / healing reaction I have provoked was a psychotic episode in a schizophrenic. Unfortunately, due to the severity of the reaction, the matter was then taken out of my hands, no doubt to be managed with pharmaceuticals. Although I can absolutely see the necessity of this approach in the circumstances, I can only wonder and hope that the person was able to find a way to progress with the deeper healing that was required.

In my experience, however intense and uncomfortable the detox is, it is always worth persevering.

FORGIVENESS - AN ESSENTIAL ASPECT OF HEALING

Detoxing the inner environment is significantly more complex as much of the mental and emotional load is out of reach. Often the patient has been carrying it around for so long they don't fully recognise it's there, they don't think it's a problem or cannot access it, because it is locked away in the subconscious. Forgiveness seems to be one of the keys that unlocks a great deal.

Before getting in to the specifics of forgiveness, may I offer an analogy which encapsulates how I see the accumulation of inner toxins:

Imagine a beautiful glass made of the most exquisite crystal, placed on a high mountain where the snow and ice is melting in the sunshine and filling it with meltwater. The sun streams through the crystal and sparkles through the purest water which is naturally available.

The glass represents your body, the water is your natural purity, and the sunlight is the Love which is flowing through you all the time. As you are enlivened by the Love, it makes you sparkle.

Now imagine putting some grit or mud into the glass. It is a pollutant. It defiles the natural beauty. In time it will settle to the bottom, giving the appearance that the water is clear, but it is rapidly stirred up by any agitation. This is akin to the process of bringing negative mental or emotional pollution into the body. If it is not cleared, any new negativity is going to disturb and add to the existing residue.

The pollution of beauty always offends. This is what makes people with a lot of negativity unattractive. If I am negative in response, it can also make me unattractive too. Such is the result of judgment.

My challenge is to accept others as they truly are – to see the crystal glass and not the mud. In relation to forgiveness, this means that the first step is a change in attitude; a willingness to look anew and see something different. It is typically only after this mental shift that a whole-hearted emotional transformation can happen.

HOW TO FORGIVE

A caveat before starting this section – there is no magic formula for forgiveness. Your way of forgiving is not going to be the same as mine. However, I'd like to share my own process, with the intention of prompting a few ideas. You may just find something that helps you get started.

When I have reached a point of readiness to forgive, I create a setting of peace. I make sure that all phones are switched off and any other likely disturbances are minimised. If anyone rings the doorbell, I will not answer it during this time. Otherwise, the house is empty.

I light a candle. I might play some uplifting music.

I then sit, become as relaxed as possible and I say aloud in the room:

"Now I am going to forgive two people. One is... for saying/doing things which I found hurtful, and the second person is me for feeling bitter/angry/hurt about what was said/done." (I use specific words to convey the exact thing that has been said or done and the emotion that I have been holding).

Then I wait in silence. I still my mind and feel for the moment when my heart is ready, when my words are *heart-felt*. I feel deeply ready to forgive. With this compassion and Love I bring... to mind; I can see them in my mind's eye.

From deep in my heart, I say "I forgive you". I *feel* the true meaning of that phrase. I then watch their reaction in my mind's eye. Everyone is different. When first visualised, they may be scowling, angry or aloof or expressing any other emotion. After the forgiveness they may smile, or dance, or open arms to you, or bow, moving with lightness, grace and gratitude. They may turn and walk away. This may signal that they are moving out of my life or that they see this as the opportunity to consider this matter closed, leaving us both free to move on.

Then, still feeling the heartfelt intensity of the moment, I say" I forgive myself". I fill myself with Love, with compassion, with understanding, with tolerance, with joy, and with gratitude. I forgive myself for my vulnerability, and I acknowledge my part. I wonder if I was being too proud; is that why I felt hurt? Did I have expectations which were not justified (are they ever)? I aim to uncover a deeper truth about my reaction, and allow this deeper understanding to sink in. I may also contemplate the other person's actions more deeply, seeking compassionate understanding.

When I understand their past I understand their reactions. In my mind, I ask them to forgive my previous lack of understanding. All I can do is to endlessly forgive their attitudes, feelings, thoughts, words and actions where these were based on fear. From deep in my heart of hearts I repeat "I forgive, I forgive, I forgive."

Then I have gratitude for the whole event. I realise it illustrated my own lack of a particular aspect of Love. I thank them for this precious insight. I then let whatever emotions are within me come to the surface and escape; as tears of release and relief or joy, as smiles, as laughter or simply as a profound sense of peace.

Finally I thank myself in appreciation of this whole moment of living and learning, growing and moving on.

There is a test of forgiveness.

When the person you have forgiven next comes to mind, what is your reaction to them? Do you feel angry or tense in some way? Do you feel warm, compassionate, understanding and tolerant towards them?

If you feel angry and tense you haven't fully forgiven, you only think you have. If you feel compassionate and noticeably softer then your forgiveness is true and complete. You know when forgiveness has been successful because there is no longer any emotional charge associated with the event or the person should you ever call either of these to mind.

If you try this test and realise you haven't truly forgiven don't beat yourself up over it; simply make the realisation, accept it and resolve to repeat the process of forgiveness from deep in your heart of hearts.

Why not do it right now?

Sadly, many people feel unworthy of forgiveness and so find it difficult to forgive themselves for some past thought or action. Part of the healing process is the realisation that there is no value in holding onto guilt, the only value is in the learning. In a culture brought up to fear and with the notion of sin and therefore guilt, the concept of forgiveness is often difficult to understand.

I've come to believe that the only sin is to act against the dictates of your Soul, because then you act against not only your own best interests but also against the best interests of those around you. Universal healing energy transcends right and wrong and therefore eclipses sin and guilt. There is no duality at this level, only wisdom and knowing and the realisation that every ego has to learn.

When you are truly ready, forgiveness happens in an instant because of the integrity of the intention. You immediately feel lighter and more joyful because a major burden has been shed. You may release a torrent of tears or laugh or smile with delight as you let go of the huge weight of guilt and unworthiness that you have carried, perhaps for years. With this relief comes the realisation that you are not beneath forgiveness. No one is. You will also find it much easier to forgive others once you have forgiven yourself. This forgiveness may be of an organisation which has caused hurt in any way in the past. The hold certain people or organisations had on you in the past has been relinquished. You are now free to move on. If someone has a hold on you from the past, it is influencing your present, which is changing your future. By breaking this hold your present is immediately changed, as will be your future. This whole approach may seem crazy to some people. All I can tell you is that it works and is fundamental to all complete healing.

Let me illustrate it with just one example.

Peggy had been coming to see me for some 3 years. Every time I saw her I kept finding suppressed resentment, and with it a significantly increased risk of developing breast cancer, yet she adamantly denied that the resentment could even possibly exist. One time I saw her, the only finding I could make was of resentment. This time, I was much more direct in my approach, urging her to share anything that she could think of that may explain her resentment. At last she agreed. Peggy recounted that she had been having a feud with a person, let's call her Joan, for over 25 years. The reasons for the feud had been lost in the mists of lang syne (the long since). I suggested the only thing she could do would be to go straight home and, in a setting of undisturbable peace, bring Joan to mind and forgive her from deep in her heart. She did that on the Thursday. The following Sunday she happened to be at an afternoon social gathering. What should happen but Joan was there, who came across to Peggy and said something to the effect:"Isn't it time we stopped this carry on? We've wasted so much time on this in the past. Let's let bygones be bygones and forget it."

That's exactly what happened. That's what they did. They both felt better for it. Not only that but when I next tested Peggy she had no signs of resentment. I did the test, told her I could find absolutely nothing and said that whatever she had done had worked. Then she told me the story above. Coincidence? Of course it could be – but after 25 years of ingrained attitudes and thought patterns? Cause and effect? Of course it could be. Does it matter which? I don't believe so. The important outcome for me was twofold: the patient healed completely; Joan also experienced some measure of healing. Two people benefited from one person's forgiveness.

THE FOUR STAGES OF HEALING

I stated in the introduction that each person's journey into and out of illness is unique. However, one of the great gifts afforded by thousands of hours of experience is the ability to take an overview and recognise common patterns. What has emerged are three distinct patterns of healing, which happen irrespective of the age of the client and the stage of the illness.

As you see from the graph the slope rises from bottom left to top right, from illness towards wellness.

Progress of Healing

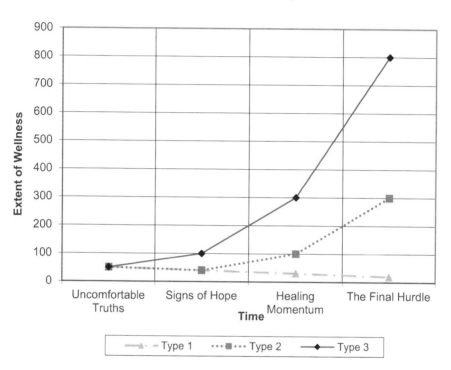

The typical trajectory of each of the three types is indicated as a straight line between the points, but in reality there are usually many ups and downs along the way.

I am going to describe each of the stages on the healing pathway. Plainly the divisions between the stages are somewhat arbitrary. Also, how long a patient stays in one stage before they move on to the next seems completely idiosyncratic and unpredictable.

Therefore, the total time it takes for health to be re-established is exactly as long as a piece of string, as well as being nebulous, fun, challenging, frustrating, humbling, erratic, even appearing to be random on occasion.

STAGE 1 – UNCOMFORTABLE TRUTHS

This is the most confusing time for the patient.

For the first time they become aware of all the factors or toxins (that are accessible at this time) which are contributing to their illness, and there can be a sense of overload.

Their old patterns of thinking, feeling, reacting, eating, sleeping, exercising are thrown into question. The notion of their home – their sanctuary and refuge – being a possible contributor to their illness through e.g. geopathic stress or the toxic effect of electronic technology is fundamentally unsettling and unnerving.

In this first stage, there are three types of personal response:

TYPE 1

'I don't believe all this. The therapist has not described me at all [denial and rationalisation]. I'm going to ignore it and keep on doing my own thing'.

If they choose not to engage with the necessary lifestyle changes at this stage, they will remain stuck in their illness pattern which will become inexorably more deeply imprinted. A person with this approach will follow the bottom line on the graph, unless they make further change.

Although disbelief may be their initial reaction, it may be that after a period of reflection (which sometimes can last for years), they choose to come back or go to another therapist and start again. If this is the case, they may well shift to Type 2. However, they will probably start lower down on the vertical axis and their progress is likely to take longer through each stage because their condition is more deeply embedded.

TYPE 2

The clients who follow this pattern are typically more open-minded and/or their motivation for healing outweighs their scepticism. Their thought pattern is often along the lines of 'This seems like a crazy amount of stuff to think about. It's not what I expected but I'm willing to give it a try for a short time and see how I go'.

A significant number of 'Type 1' and 'Type 2' patients have major difficulties because they have been weaned on the notion of 'a pill for every ill'. They assume their doctor must know the causes of the illness and that the pills will do the trick. Ten years later the doctor is still prescribing pills, the patient still has symptoms. Culturally and conceptually this approach is bankrupt and the patient is paying for it in so many ways.

Rarely is the notion of the patient taking responsibility for themselves expressed or expected.

TYPE 3

Now the patient is fully ready and willing to face a whole change of emphasis, from being passive receivers of approaches designed to control their symptoms, to becoming active participants in the guardianship of their wellness.

Getting their heads and attitudes around to accepting this is a major challenge but one that they readily take on. Those who fit the 'Type 3' pattern are the ones whose attitude is,

'Wow! What a lot of stuff! I'm absolutely committed and am going to go all out and see what happens.'

The trajectory of the top line on the graph is therefore only possible for those who fully embrace all that is needed.

In summary, the patient's initial response to the 'Uncomfortable Truths' stage will establish their most likely trajectory. As they take the first few steps towards their healing, the patient begins to get glimpses of normal health. Initially these may last for just moments. As they continue to do what they need to do, these glimpses become longer in duration and more frequent in occurrence.

Also during this phase all symptoms relating to food intolerance can get very much worse. As a general rule here: the younger the client, the shorter the worsening.
I remember a little girl I treated who was 4 years old at the time. Her eczema became dramatically worse for 10 days, when she began excluding milk products from her diet completely.

Afterwards she said, "It was as if my body was pushing something out through my skin."

I have to say that today I have no better nor simpler way of describing that process of detoxification. Fourteen days after she was first seen you would never know that this wee lassie had had eczema at all.

Still in the first stage, the patient starts to come to terms with the need to be living a different life. They have been made aware of the range of toxins affecting them including food intolerances, so realise that their buying and eating habits need to change. This is often another of the 'Uncomfortable Truths' they have to face. They always need support to address their mental and emotional issues (I use the Bach Flower Remedies for this), and may also need some nutritional supplements. They may start to become more aware of changes within themselves in terms of their energy levels, aches and pains, sleep patterns, concentration span, old emotional hurts, the need for forgiveness and many other things. Knowing what they need to change is a major step forward from having symptoms but not knowing why they are there.

As each little improvement registers within them they become more motivated to continue along this different path.

Unfortunately in this first stage, the bad days may still outnumber the good and the bad times tend to last longer than the good. But as the days go by an improvement is becoming gradually more noticeable as each good period lengthens.

Often there is enough change happening here to help the patient to realise that something is going on. Usually the whole spectrum of their presenting symptoms re-appears in one way or another. Initially these can be more severe but tend to be more transient than of old.

The more these symptoms diminish in quality and quantity, the more encouraged the patient becomes to continue along this new path.

At least this change is, usually, something new for them in their illness experience. Previously they have probably endured a slow, progressive limitation to their functioning. This is often accompanied by pain which, again, is likely to have increased gradually in frequency, duration and intensity over time.

STAGE 2 – Signs Of Hope

During this stage the detoxing is continuing while healing is beginning. Many processes are going on in parallel in the body at any one time.

Here the patient is beginning to trust the process more as they feel improvement in many areas of their lives. They become willing to explore their underlying mental and emotional issues and are starting to get used to the new nutritional pattern dictated by their food intolerances. Their confidence in managing themselves has grown.

This also has the wonderful effect of helping them realise that they, and they alone, are responsible for their own health, and that what they do or don't do can have an immediate effect on them. Usually they embrace this. From having been the passive recipient of prescribed pharmaceuticals, to taking control is a major step.

As clients experience more glimpses of wellness, confidence continues to grow. This confidence mirrors the continuing diminution in duration, frequency and severity of their original symptoms. Their energy, concentration, appetite, quality of sleep, temperament, vitality, libido, sense of fun are all improving.

Still the bad moments may outnumber the good in terms of frequency, duration and severity but they have enough experience and awareness now to embrace the changes within them and they know what they have to do as an individual to keep making progress.

STAGE 3 – Healing Momentum

The margin between stages 2 and 3 is the point at which the good periods and the bad are equal in number, frequency, duration and severity.

This is usually evident in retrospect.

The patient now really has a sense of healing momentum. They are becoming much more enthusiastic. They can feel the rewards of their necessary self-discipline, deeper self-awareness and empowerment. They know they are moving forwards. They have more energy, are more engaged with life, lighter (more buoyant), have a greater sense of fun. They have better sleep. They will often have lost weight. (One lady lost five and a half stones, i.e. 77 lbs., in 18 months simply by sticking with her food exclusions).

[As an aside here: I believe that most gross obesity is due to non-awareness of food intolerance. See the A-Z].

They will also have had a few, usually innocent, lapses in their nutrition and slips into old behaviours but, being more self-aware, they are conscious of the link between repeating old habits and the return of old symptoms.

The difference between their old self and the new is really being felt. The parallel changes in the physical, mental and emotional levels are accumulating. There is no way they want to go backwards from here.

In this phase the diminution of frequency, duration and severity of symptoms continues. But each symptom return acts as a reminder of the need to continue with the self-awareness and discipline that has got them this far. The pathway to healing is never a straight line. As long as the general trend is towards healing, any downers need to be experienced and seen as impermanent, frustrating though that can be. They know that they need to simply ride out the storm and that the sun will shine again soon.

Towards the end of this stage, the number of good days increasingly outnumbers the bad days.

STAGE 4 – THE FINAL HURDLE

Here the good days are the norm. The patient feels almost fully fit. Their illness is just a bad memory. But something paradoxical happens. When a bad day occurs, it seems to hit really hard.

The blow is as much psychological as physical. But it is felt so deeply that they question whether they have wasted all their time and effort to date. Even though the majority of the days are good, the power of the bad day rocks them on their heels.

Their classic thought is:

"Oh my God, it (the illness) is coming back."

There is a feeling almost of devastation as their mind-talk rattles on about:

"What a waste of time and effort... I'm as bad as I ever was... I'm just going to get worse again...etc."

At this time they need courage and perseverance and support and reassurance, because their levels of doubt and dismay are enormous.

I see this stage as a reminder to the patient that the process is continuing, that there is a need for more healing to embed in the system. It is also a timely illustration of how ill they were to start with. Curiously people forget how poorly they used to be.

Once the last vestiges of illness have played out, then they are flying!

When I first see a patient, I often suggest they have a photograph taken of themselves that day, date it, write their weight on the back, and put it away somewhere. Then I suggest that in a year's time they should have another photo done, take out the old picture and compare it with the new.

Often their improvement doesn't take a year, but this suggestion gives them a notion of the time and commitment they need. It also reduces the impatience that so impedes healing. (Maybe it is no coincidence that those who seek a doctor's advice are called patients!).

In summary, these are the fundamental four stages I have seen in the healing pathway over the years. Actually I think the graph is not a straight line but shows an exponential rise. Given what I've learned from the multiple models of health and healing that I have studied, this makes sense. As more parts of more systems detoxify and so function more effectively then the multitude of systems they support and iterate with improve accordingly. Those systems in turn become more effective and iterate with multitudes more, hence the exponential progress.

It is worth restating that the duration, severity and frequency of these phases is utterly individual and well worth the effort *eventually*.

However, unless you are determined to become well and are prepared to do everything you can to achieve that, I would suggest you don't even start. It is hard work, especially to begin with, yet the results are life-changing. [See client stories in the '*In Their Own Write*' chapter].

CONVALESCENCE

Convalescence may be necessary after any condition until the body's energies are fully restored to normal. Many people try to shorten the convalescent phase but that is often short-sighted and counter-productive. In my experience this phase is very important for all the systems in the body to return to their normal, healthy activity. The key to the return to normal is often the amount of energy felt by the person. If the energy is subnormal, this is a clear indication that more convalescence is required.

I always advise people that they need to feel completely normal in every way for at least one day before they go back to work/school/college.

The logic behind this is: if recuperating patients return to work feeling 80% better, they can only do 80% of what they were used to doing. The next day they can still only function at 80% yet the additional 20% or their workload from yesterday still has to be processed. Being only at 80% efficiency means there is another deficit of 20% of the workload for today, which adds to yesterday's deficit. These add up to the point where tomorrow they are facing 140% of their workload, with only 80% of their energy. The accumulated deficits mean that the struggle increases day-by-day, leading to exhaustion and the possibility of needing months off work to allow for complete recovery.

Consider this a well-meaning finger wagging at you from out of the page – trying to be a hero and returning to work too soon is always counter-productive, both for the employee and the employer.

THE ROLE OF SLEEP

Repair and healing of tissue happens in deep delta sleep. This is why people need more sleep during the healing phases from illness. Going without sleep is unnatural, and harmful in the long term. It also leads to poor performance in all areas of life.

Persistent lack of sleep leads to insufficient tissue repair and healing.

Insomnia is repeated lack of quality, deep sleep. People with long-term insomnia have more likelihood of developing illness early because their bodies have a reduced amount of the deep delta phase of sleep. This kind of sleep is both nourishing and correcting so when it is compromised, people will heal more slowly. As people detox, typically their sleep pattern improves, as does their overall energy and quality of life.

One of my clients with sleep apnoea reported that his apparatus was recording more than 40 episodes of apnoea per night when I first saw him. Six weeks later, he was down to 15, and two months after that, it was down to 4 or 5.

LOVE AND HEALING

I find that no true healing happens until the person loves themselves enough and is sufficiently passionate about their reason for living to have the discipline to change their habits of thinking, judging, accepting, forgiving, nutrition and exercise. These are what change the internal environment.

They also value themselves enough to change their external environment as much as they can such that their domestic and workplace energies are conducive to health and are not supporting illness.

Generating serenity within and being in a nourishing environment is the perfect remedy to enable healing.

It is simple, but definitely not easy.

THE FUNDAMENTAL TRUTH ABOUT HEALTH: REVEALING THE ULTIMATE SECRET OF THE SCOTTISH WITCH DOCTOR

I accept that my clinic, in parts, does have the appearance of a mad professor's workshop. There are unfamiliar pieces of machinery, some of which crackle, bleep and fizz. And when I do my testing, it is all a mystery to the client as to how I come up with the findings that I do. When they ask me 'How does this work?' I enigmatically reply 'By magic'.

However unconventional it all is, sometimes client's aches and pains disappear almost instantaneously or conditions they've had for decades begin to recover. Yet, the real secret is very simple – it's all about frequencies. 'Everything is frequencies', to paraphrase Tesla and Einstein. If you're thinking 'Well that secret's no good to me, because I don't get it' let me unravel some of the mystery.

At its most fundamental, everything is energy; different kinds of energy have different frequencies. You're possibly already aware that one musical note has a different frequency to another note, and one colour of light has a different frequency to another colour. In the case of music, when several notes are played together, you have a chord of frequencies. Depending on the notes, some chords sound harmonious while others sound dissonant.

It is the same in the body. Some combinations of frequencies feel harmonious and are conducive to health, others feel jarring and are out of sync with the body's natural settings.

When we are bombarded with dissonant frequencies from the various sources mentioned in the Toxins chapter, our bodies respond by creating disease. Imagine the screeching sound of fingertips scraping down a blackboard; in response you might instinctively put your hands over your ears and make a pained expression, or even feel a visceral shudder. With more subtle forms of dissonance, this type of reaction may be going on all over your body, but in such a way that you are not conscious of it. Like a bad smell that you eventually stop noticing, you become accustomed to the dissonance and think it is normal. In fact, it **is** normal but it is not healthy. Consequently, when illness arrives you have no idea why.

Looking at health from this perspective, I believe that energetic frequencies are the future of therapeutics in Medicine. Every tissue, every organ, every cell and every substructure has its own unique frequency. Frequencies can add together, and they can neutralise or delete each other. Therefore, external frequencies can stimulate cells, organs or tissues in a healthy way, or they can interfere with normal function and therefore illness begins. Every illness has its own frequency signature. Therefore, every illness has the potential to be deleted by the precise inverted frequency signature.

The major challenge many of us face today in respect of our health is that we have completely lost touch with how it feels to be fully in tune with our natural, healthy frequency settings. Although we instinctively know that it feels better to be in nature, in the sunshine, and in peaceful, happy and relaxed company, daily pollution of all kinds has become so commonplace that we accept it unquestioningly.

All the gadgets I have, the techniques I use and the remedies I offer (e.g. Homeopathy and Flower Essences) have one core aim – to re-establish the flow of healthy energies. As I just mentioned, at times the impact of doing this is immediate, though more often than not, it takes time for any such frequency changes to translate to lasting change in the body. The other main issue is that the clients have to understand about how to create this for themselves. There's no point in expecting me (or anyone else for that matter) to fix a problem, if they are going to walk out of the appointment, straight back in to the old problematic and dissonant frequencies i.e. in the same toxic atmosphere with the same toxic thoughts and emotions, and eating the same toxic foods.

BECOMING YOUR OWN WITCH DOCTOR

In the introduction, I stated that one of my main aims in writing the book was for you to be able to take back control of your health, rather than leave it totally in others' hands. If any of what you have read has been inspiring or thought provoking for you, and you want to know what you can do to become your own witch doctor, I can assure you that a lot of it is beautifully simple.

If you can fill yourself and your life with the following, it will make a huge difference:

- an energetically clean environment
- non-toxic nutrition
- exercise in clean fresh air
- a deep sense of connection with a partner, family, friends, pets or a community
- a sense of humour
- relaxation and self-nourishment, by engaging in enjoyable and fulfilling pursuits
- appreciation of the interconnectedness of everything
- gratitude for how Mother Nature supports us in so many ways
- profound acceptance

The cleaner you become, the clearer you become. As you increasingly rid yourself of toxins, and your whole being resumes its natural flow, you become more sensitive and begin to know intuitively what feels good – whether this is in the domain of relationships, the places you spend your time in, the kind of activities you chose or the types of food you eat. You just know what's right for you and what is not. This is the way to become truly in control of your wellbeing.

I've talked at length about food, but one final thought on this – it seems that human bodies have not evolved to digest processed foods, industrially farmed wheat, dairy products, caffeine and refined sugar. You'd be surprised how many different expressions of this I've seen.

Karen, a woman in her 40s came to me with chronic back pain and severe stiffness. Over 10 years, she'd been to multiple specialists including Chiropractors and Osteopaths. Despite numerous manipulations, nothing had had a lasting effect. Although I also do spinal manipulation for back pain when needed, I felt there was no point in repeating what had already been done. Instead, I focused on exploring Karen's whole health. Again, I discovered she had a strong adverse reaction to dairy products. Ten days after our appointment, having cut these out of her diet completely, Karen phoned me to say that she had just washed her hair leaning over the wash hand basin. She had been unable to do this for more than a decade due to the lack of flexibility in her back. She had no pain and no further stiffness.

I can only reiterate that once we stop these foods many illnesses just melt away and, metabolically, we get younger and healthier, and have more energy.

Going back to the list of simple health-promoting frequencies, profound acceptance is typically the most difficult, yet the most impactful. To begin to address this, let's dip back in to the subject of mental and emotional toxins.

What I've found is that, at the root of a lot of illness, is an emotionally painful event in infancy or young childhood which we were not equipped to deal with at that age. The emotions we were unable to process then recur at different times through later life, like a ball that bounces over long distances of time and place.

Each bounce provides an opportunity to reflect on these emotions and these reflections serve either to alleviate the underlying distress or embed it. When negative judgment is added, the toxic soup becomes ever more bitter and the resulting pattern of frequencies ever more pathological. In other words, the emotions, the lack of acceptance, the judgement and the lack of forgiveness remain in our system as toxic energies.

As we get older and hopefully wiser, we come to realise that our judgement is making things worse. Two things then need to happen: the first is to stop judging, simply accept events with no emotional charge; and the second is to forgive ourselves for our litany of judgements. Acceptance of events and applying wisdom along with non-attachment to the outcome leads to inner peace.

Once we have forgiven everybody who has hurt us in whatever way and recognise that all they have done is to contribute to our learning, and we get to the point where we genuinely can thank them, inner peace will soar.

It is as if the whole of life leads us to the point of simple acceptance and unconditional forgiveness, both of ourselves and of others.

The great thing is, every part of this is in *your* control.

Remember, the Human Being has an astonishing ability to heal itself. This means that YOU have an extraordinary ability to heal. As I have said, I believe that everything has the potential to be reversed. Do you?

It is never too late to begin.

It is my heartfelt hope that you come to know that Love from the Universe is flowing through you at all times. Ultimately it is Love that heals everybody of everything.

May I introduce you to the Health Equation:

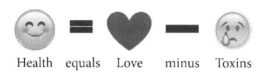

Health equals Love minus Toxins

So your health is the resultant of the Love, flowing to you, through you and from you, minus all the toxins be they physical, emotional, mental or spiritual.

Life has ease, not dis-ease, when you take down the barriers that prevent Love from flowing, The inner peace is amazing.

As Walt Whitman says in his wonderful poem 'Leaves of Grass':

"*Discard whatever insults your Soul.*"

May you celebrate the health you have, and do all that you possibly can to enhance it. Have no reservations about asking others to help you in this quest. You are worth it. Most people are delighted to be asked to provide help in whichever way it is needed.

The ultimate aim is to reach the point where the Health Equation has zero after the minus sign. Therefore you will smile radiantly because you're are filled with Love; your Heart is full.

May you maximise your Health!

PART THREE

FOR
REFERENCE

The Disclaimer is repeated here lest you have turned straight to this section. I can only speak from my experience which, of course, may not apply to you.

THE A-Z:
AN ORGANON OF CURRENT MEDICAL CONDITIONS

An Organon is defined as an instrument of thought or knowledge.

What follows is my collection of findings, illness by illness, based on seeing many, many clients with a vast range of conditions. Of course, I haven't seen all medical conditions, but those I have seen have added to my experience and knowledge, so enabling me to apply that learning to more people. As I keep learning and evolving, I accept that all my current beliefs and knowledge are subject to change.

I would also like to reiterate that I always treat people, never conditions. This Organon is purely for reference and represents only a starting point from which a thorough personal exploration of illness can begin.

ACNE

This is usually caused by refined sugars, chocolate, coffee, cola, cocoa, often with dairy products as well. Excluding the offending foods is usually sufficient to see a complete reversal of Acne.

In women, Acne is often associated with Pre-Menstrual Tension, [PMT], and other period problems (see later).

The underlying emotions are usually fear, indicating the presence of something they cannot face.

ADDICTION

All narcotic and alcohol addiction can be halted within 10 days. In that time it is possible for the body's biochemistry to return to the pre-narcotic state.

The technique that enables this has been available since the 1970s and it was devised Dr Meg Patterson who called it 'NeuroElectricTherapy', or NET for short.

During NET any cravings usually disappear on or by Day 4. Cocaine, Heroin, Methamphetamine usually need only 6 days of 24 hour a day treatment. Alcohol and Methadone take 8-10 days, as do anti-depressants. It is rare for any addiction to need more than 10 days of treatment, all without needing pharmaceuticals.

Once the Addiction has been reversed then the client is amenable to counselling to treat the underlying emotional pain, such as: lack of self-worth, major grief, a sense of betrayal, deep anger/rage from which the Addict is trying to numb themselves. That process will likely take much longer.

A philanthropist, bless you whoever you are, gave some money to look at the effectiveness of NET in Scotland. The project became ScotNET. Between 2010 and 2014 I was Medical Adviser to ScotNET.

There were only 4 of us in the team and we had no facility by which I mean we had no hospital ward nor residential space that we could use exclusively for this project. We had to send people to the Republic of Ireland or to the North of Scotland to facilities which were often religious in tone and nature. That tone did not suit many of the Addicts but that was all we had available to us. Despite our small size and lack of dedicated resources we treated 1% of the registered addict population of Scotland in that time. The NET was applied for up to 10 days, depending on the narcotics used by the Addicts, followed by Counselling. If my memory serves, the proved abstinence rate 6 months after NET was of the order of 60%, and the average treatment time was 8 days, all without pharmaceuticals.

Previous experience with NET when proper facilities are in place and trained counsellors are available, takes the success rate to more than 80%.

In comparison, the Government's own figures for the success of Methadone, now decades old, is 3%. Why would anyone tolerate a waste of 97%?

Norman Stone's film about NET called: 'The Final Fix', narrated by Ewan McGregor, is well worth watching.

I thought we had proved the value of NET and, frankly, thought that the Scottish Government would continue the program, allowing us to have our own dedicated facilities and personnel.

This did not happen, for reasons I cannot fathom.

What other technique is as simple, as versatile and as effective in so short a time? I can think of none.

Who or what influenced the politicians?

Why are Addicts not getting effective treatment? Why are their needs not being met?

Are they not worthy of great assistance in returning to being responsible members of society?

The whole of Society would benefit. Less criminality, less police and court time, prisons less crowded. Why does the government not want this?

NET is astonishingly effective, and having worked closely with it for a number of years, I am deeply saddened by the way Addiction has been widely treated.

Investigative journalism would (I expect) find a myriad of stories underlying the non-use of NET. It would seem the politicians and policy makers with the influence to change things are all too often influenced more heavily by the businesses with the most money and power, than the ones with the most potential.

Scotland has the highest rate of deaths from narcotic use, which I find unnecessary, even shameful. Dr Meg Paterson was Scottish. Her invention has been available since the mid 1970s. The number of people globally who could have benefitted from it is uncountable.

In my view, investigation has to be carried out to show why the NICE, the FDA, indeed every assessor of medical equipment, has been so inert in accepting NET. The costs to society will continue to be huge if no new approaches to addiction are implemented.

ALOPECIA

Suppressed resentment proved to be a powerful underlying driver of this auto-immune condition in every person with Alopecia that I have seen. Other common underlying emotions were anger, hatred and grief.

ANKYLOSING SPONDYLITIS

The patient usually has very similar food intolerances to those with Rheumatoid Arthritis (mostly dairy products and wheat).

The pains suffered by this group when withdrawing from the rogue foods is the most severe of any group that I have seen. Indeed none of them have managed their pain sufficiently to want to continue with these exclusions. So to date I have never had significant success in helping anyone with Ankylosing Spondylitis reverse their condition. However, it's been many years since I've seen anyone with this and now that I have more knowledge regarding pain management, I maintain that reversal is still possible.

Suppressed emotions: dogmatic, inflexible, judgemental, can't bear something in life, great fear.

ARTERIAL DISEASE (ARTERIOSCLEROSIS)

My finding is that refined sugar is virtually always a toxin as is caffeine, coffee, cola, cocoa and chocolate. Milk and its products are usually also not tolerated by those with this condition.

I remember a man who came to see me, who could only walk 100 yards before the pain in his calf muscles stopped him. Narrowing of his arteries meant that these muscles were not getting enough oxygen. He also had erectile dysfunction and he had not had sex for the previous 10 years.

At his third visit, some 9 weeks after the first consultation, he was walking very much further, plus he had had sex twice in the previous month. I think I said 'So that means that two of you were smiling!'

ASTHMA

An acute asthma attack is like drowning in fresh air, you just cannot get another breath. I say this from personal experience. When visiting dear friends in Amsterdam I became increasingly wheezy to the point where I needed hospital admission. The paramedic ambulance crew were amazing and it was flashing blue lights at high speed through the city. All because I had an allergy to cats, something I had been completely unaware of.

Yet this is not just due to inhaled toxins. Again, in my experience foodstuffs can play a major role, especially milk. This is particularly the case when someone is somewhat overweight and has indigestion or constipation or any of the other components of irritable bowel syndrome.

Another feature of Asthmatics is their historical suppression of emotions. They are often too frightened to speak.

I remember seeing a boy of 12 who weighed 15 and a half stones. He was asthmatic. I think I only saw him once. Some 4 months later his father phoned to ask me when would his son's weight loss stop. I assured him that the weight loss would plateau and then he would enter a growth spurt which duly happened. I think he got down to about 9 stones before gaining weight healthily. He reacted badly to cow's milk and all its products.

Suppressed emotions: frightened to express themselves, grief.

BRAIN BALANCE

The technical name for brain balance, where there is an appropriate balance of functioning in both hemispheres of the brain, is *Laterality*. Laterality is normal when the left brain is dominant in a right-handed person; conversely the right brain is dominant in a left-handed person.

Laterality is abnormal in most people with a chronic condition. Their ability to deal with stress, pain and distress is much reduced, as is their ability to heal, when laterality is abnormal.

In my experience laterality can be either completely abnormal or what I term 'crossed'.

In abnormal laterality the right brain is dominant in a right-handed individual while in a left-hander the left brain is dominant.

I class the laterality as 'crossed' when the ability to calculate is normal yet the testing shows that the wrong hemisphere is still dominant. It can be the other way round: the correct hemisphere is in charge while the ability to calculate is wrong.

The value of correcting this is difficult to quantify though it definitely serves to restore the normal healthy flow of energy in the body and, therefore, is an important part of returning to health. Pain can sometimes disappear instantly once the laterality has been corrected. When I was a GP (General Practitioner) I remember a man coming in on crutches. He had broken his leg 6 weeks before and that morning had gone back to the hospital to have the plaster cast removed. He still had pain afterwards and was told to get painkillers.

I checked his laterality, it was squint (abnormal). I corrected it and he walked out with no pain, carrying his crutches, and he had no need for analgesics.

CANCER

In 2005 I got a phone call from a dear friend. He said: "Roger there is a cure for cancer."

I have to confess my cynicism sparked up straightaway. By that time in my career I had heard many claims about many diseases, none of which ever came to fruition, and maybe age does bring a slightly more cynical view.

He went on to tell me about the work of Professor Gerry Potter in the University of Leicester. So I telephoned Professor Potter. There's nothing like the direct approach.

Professor Potter told me about his work with very specific fruit extracts. He calls them 'Salvestrols', from Salve, to save i.e. the same root as Salvation.

At the suggestion of Prof Potter I talked with one of his lab assistants. The lab assistant told me that he had a neighbour who had prostate cancer. PSA stands for Prostate-

Specific Antigen and it is a blood test used as a marker for the level of prostate cancer activity. The neighbour's PSA was 2400. I had never heard of levels more than 400 before, anything up to 4 is normal. This man had liver secondaries (a secondary is a deposit of cancer tissue distant from the first cancerous tissue, which is called the primary), lung secondaries, brain secondaries and spinal secondaries. His Oncologist told him there was nothing more he could do, to get his affairs in order and to enjoy the last couple of months of his life. The lab assistant asked Professor Potter for permission to give Salvestrols to his neighbour. After a month his PSA was around 400. After three or four months his PSA was normal and he went back to the Oncologist who was surprised to see him. On hearing the story about his drop in PSA the consultant arranged for a repeat of the scans. There were no signs of any cancer in any of the tissues that showed secondaries or primary cancer previously.

That story really convinced me, and I have been recommending Salvestrols since 2006 to everyone for whom it is appropriate.

The key to the effectiveness of this treatment is that there is a particular enzyme in at least 80% of all cancer cells. This enzyme is known as Cytochrome P450 CYP1B1. It is now recognised as a universal cancer marker.

When Salvestrol washes across a cell which has CYP1 B1 in it the Salvestrol is broken down, and what it breaks down into is toxic for that cell. So that cancer cell dies. The healthy cells are untouched. So it is highly targeted natural chemotherapy made from very particular fruit extracts.

The benefits of Salvestrol:

- it will work in every cell that has CYP1 B1 i.e. more than 80% of cancer cell types.

- Healthy cells stay healthy; there is no known collateral damage.
- there are no known side-effects.
- they are extracted from widely available fruits.
- they are cheap, some £60 for a tub of 90 capsules, in comparison to the thousands of pounds charged for chemotherapy agents.
- they are taken by mouth; they do not have to be given by infusion.

NB I have seen at least one case in which the impact of high doses of Salvestrol, 8 capsules per day, was neutralised by the intense stress experienced by a client, both professionally and personally. Professionally they had to work under extraordinary stress for four months of the year, denied any time off during that spell and having mandatory deadlines to meet. Instead of retiring in the month before this interval they thought they would 'help out' their employer through this busy time. Putting the needs of others before yours when your own being is crying out for help, and putting income before health, is never a healthy equation. This also emphasised to me the primal importance of emotions and stress as the fundamental drivers of cancer, indeed of all illnesses.

Professor Potter realised that to get them available through conventional trials would take 14 to 15 years. He said he could not bear the thought of those who would suffer unnecessarily in that time and realised that, because they are not pharmaceuticals, they can be sold as food or nutritional supplements. So that is how they are sold.

I typically now recommend these alongside my usual whole-health approach to determine other contributory factors to the cancer.

CHOLESTEROL

There has been a massive focus on cholesterol in the last 60 years. Is it justified?

Blood vessels have their own puncture repair kit.

If there is a leak from a blood vessel a reaction occurs at the site of the leak in which a patch of cholesterol seals the blood vessel, so preventing further blood loss. This patch arises from the Low Density Lipoproteins (L DL) which have acquired the name 'Bad Cholesterol'.

The 'Good Cholesterol' is High Density Lipoproteins (HDL) which is the cholesterol that is going back to the liver for storage. How can it be bad for a patch of cholesterol to stop someone bleeding to death?

The problem is that these patches can build up and eventually block a blood vessel which might result in a heart attack or a stroke. Or this build-up could reduce the blood supply to a busy muscle and be unable to provide enough oxygen or nutrients to that muscle; in the case of the heart muscle that would produce angina.

How can cholesterol be the Demon here?

Yes, cholesterol is *associated* with leaky arteries. Does it cause those leaks? No.

There are lots of police at a site of criminal activity. Are the police the cause of the crime? No. Are they *associated* with the crimes? Yes.

Similarly, there are a lot of fire fighters at the site of a fire. Are they the cause of the fire? No. Are they *associated* with the fires? Yes.

Association is *not* causation.

Somehow we have been persuaded that cholesterol is causative in heart disease and strokes.

That is the problem with propaganda. It is close enough to the truth to be credible, yet distant enough to be dangerous. Propaganda is only produced by those with a vested interest in the success of their message.

Pfizer's cholesterol-lowering drug Lipitor was introduced in 1997. Sales surpassed $125 billion over the lifetime of its patent. The whole food industry has been changed to provide low cholesterol this and low-fat that. If someone has high cholesterol that means they have multiple leaky arteries. What needs to be addressed is: what is causing those arteries to leak?

My understanding is that the major cause of leaky arteries is refined sugars. Yudkin told the world this in 1972 when he published his book: 'Pure, White and Deadly.' He was ridiculed, yet he was right.

CHRONIC FATIGUE

I have found that a deep emotional issue between the patient and a very close relative is at the root of all Chronic Fatigue cases I have seen. Typically, this is someone in the direct bloodline – a parent, sibling, grandparent or child.

Bear in mind that by the time people come to see me, they have usually been exhaustively investigated and any physical reasons for their illness have been excluded.

Whether perceived or real, the person does not feel loved, despite what members of the family say. They need to *feel* loved. They need hugs, they need kisses, they need reassurance by the bucket- load. They also need help to identify and treat the root causes of their issue.

Another factor has been uncovered by Dr Judy Mikovits. She published a paper in which she revealed that the majority of people with ME have a mouse retrovirus as a major contributor to the Myalgic Encephalomyelitis. The origin of the mouse retrovirus is the mouse brain tissue in which the material for some of their vaccinations was cultured.

Almost all vaccines are grown in animal tissue, which the body sees as foreign. In response to the foreign invasion, this tissue releases viruses or exosomes in due time. These viruses link with the later development of leukaemias, lymphomas and cancers in the person who has received these vaccines. In ME these viruses clatter the energy reserves of the body, making life thoroughly miserable.

In the last 10 years I have noticed an increasing number of clients who are sensitive to Wi-Fi and are drained in the presence of those vibes. Ethernet cabling from router to computer and to connected devices helps overcome this. Switching off the power to the router at night also enables much deeper, healing sleep.

I always suggest that when they feel tired, they immediately stop whatever they are doing and go have a snooze in a peaceful restful place. Their bed is ideal. They should have no agenda except to snooze and not put a time limit on this therapeutic rest. The body will awaken when it feels refreshed. Trust the body wisdom.

Suppressed emotions: fear, grief, betrayal.

CONSTIPATION

In infants, issues with digestion are usually down to food intolerance (see Irritable Bowel Syndrome), and the most common cause is the consumption of dairy products. In adults, again it can be food intolerance and a symptom of Irritable Bowel Syndrome (see below). If the constipation is a new and unfamiliar event, this signifies a change of bowel habit which demands to be further investigated so that Diverticulosis, Polyps and Cancer can be excluded.

COVID 19

I am writing this about a year into the pandemic and there is so much controversy around this virus that I find it difficult to make head or tail about what is going on. What I can tell you is what I've been suggesting to my clients and what I've been doing myself to offer the best protection. Firstly, I advise vitamin D3 (5000 units, or 125 micrograms, daily), which boosts the immune system. This is most important especially through the autumn and winter months into early spring. Take it also in the summer months if there is not much sunshine or you have not been able to get out into the fresh air. Also take a high dose of vitamin C for the same reason. No virus can survive in a high vitamin C environment. Secondly, the Bach Flower Remedy, Sweet Chestnut is strongly indicated to balance the anguish and other negativity caused by Covid-19.

Of course it is up to the individual to consider whether this is useful advice, but it is highly unlikely to do anyone any harm.

CROHN'S DISEASE

Crohn's disease can happen anywhere from the mouth to the anus. It can affect all layers of the gastrointestinal tract, which become inflamed.

In my experience, there is utterly no point in treating Crohn's disease without accurately identifying all the food intolerances and suggesting complete exclusion from these. I find the biggest culprit is dairy products, along with coffee, chocolate, cola, cocoa and refined sugar. Sometimes wheat is also a problem; occasionally it's all of them.

Also, there is little chance of long-term resolution and healing Crohn's disease unless the underlying mental and emotional issues are dealt with using a trained therapist.

Suppressed emotions: abandonment, betrayal, fear of loneliness, feeling unloved.

CROUP

I've always wondered whether Croup may not be an early sign of Asthma to come, and with the same causes. I think I have seen sufficient numbers of cases of people in the past to notice a repeating pattern, which has led me to believe that there is a strong relationship between Croup and their subsequent development of Asthma. Both seem to signal a milk intolerance.

CYSTIC FIBROSIS

I had thought that Wallach, a Vet, had explained the cause of Cystic Fibrosis back in 1978. He had fed a group of primates a diet deficient in Selenium. The clinical syndrome that this group developed had all the features of Cystic Fibrosis.

Restoring the Selenium repaired and restored their health.

I wonder why this finding is not used clinically today. Is it too simple? Why are Selenium levels not checked before and during pregnancy? Or is it a genetic inability to properly absorb and metabolise Selenium that is thought to be the underlying issue?

NB the drugs used to treat Cystic Fibrosis cost £105,000 per year. Wouldn't it be cheaper to give them Selenium capsules daily, or even a couple of brazil nuts every day?

I have never seen anyone with this condition so I have no experience regarding any potential suppressed emotions.

DEMENTIA, MULTIPLE SCLEROSIS AND MOTOR NEURONE DISEASE

I find that Mercury is the common powerful toxin in each of these groups. Those suffering from these conditions plainly have Mercury in their systems and may have a peculiar sensitivity to it. The usual source of the Mercury is the silver-coloured amalgam fillings we get at the dentist, which are 50% Mercury. The number of cases of these conditions can only reduce once the therapeutic insanity of using amalgam fillings is stopped.

In Multiple Sclerosis I find that the CytoMegalo Virus is the organism most commonly present.

Influenza vaccination: the likelihood is that people with Dementia, Multiple Sclerosis and Motor Neurone Disease are encouraged to have this vaccine regularly.

In healthy systems, the Blood Brain Barrier (which does exactly what it says) prevents any toxins in the blood from entering the brain, including heavy metals such as Mercury.

In the flu vaccine there is a component called Polysorbate. This is a detergent (why a detergent is necessary in a vaccine is beyond me). This detergent changes the properties of the blood-brain barrier in such a way that it becomes permeable to toxins including to heavy metals such as Mercury. Therefore Mercury, which is a known neurotoxin (nerve toxin), enters the brain and the nerve tissues so enhancing the progress of Dementia, Multiple Sclerosis and Motor Neurone Disease.

Another major toxin is WiFi and mobile phones. Prolonged exposure to these results in what has been called 'Digital Dementia'. Another effect of these toxins is to cause disruption of the insulating myelin sheath around nerves, so causing abnormal nerve function as seen in MS and Motor Neurone Disease. Holding a mobile phone to the head when there is a Mercury filling on the inside of that cheek probably produces more Mercury vapour which is then inhaled or swallowed, further contributing to the development of these and other conditions.

As indicated earlier, every vaccine which has a detergent in it has the ability to disrupt the blood-brain barrier and so allow the free entry of toxins into the brain. These toxins not only include heavy metals but also organisms like viruses and bacteria. So, something that is meant to be health improving, the vaccine, is in many cases, actually health depleting. Although this is becoming more widely known about, it is still immensely controversial, and the anti-vaccine lobby is much maligned.

DIABETES (TYPE 2)

In my experience this is always associated with food intolerance (see Obesity). Fundamentally Diabetics need to *zero* the dairy products and wheat that they consume. Their intolerances almost always include caffeine so that tea, coffees, chocolate, cola, cocoa have to be excluded as well as refined sugars. In adults with Diabetes, alcohol is also a major contributor.

When Diabetics have the discipline to utterly exclude all these foods the results are remarkable. Any associated Hypertension and often Irritable Bowel usually also reverse, and their blood sugar returns to normal. Then they can stop all their medication. In one Type II Diabetic who had the discipline to follow through on all the lifestyle changes, he stopped his six medications after a few months. His blood sugar and blood pressure became normal and his Irritable Bowel became a thing of the past. (His story is included in *'In Their Own Write'*).

Yet here is a curiosity: his doctor said that his Diabetes was 'in abeyance'. Does this suggest that the notion of cure is beyond consideration?

Two years after reversing his Diabetes, this client still has normal blood sugar, normal blood pressure, and needs no pharmaceuticals. He is thriving. To me his Diabetes is reversed. His condition has been cured.

My reflections on Diabetes:

- It can affect the whole body, the medical term for this is 'systemic'
- Unless all toxins are eliminated it gets worse with time, in other words it is progressive
- It seems to affect the blood supply, especially the arteries which become more and more blocked, lose their elasticity and do not function well. The medical term for this is 'arteriopathy'
- The blood sugar (glucose) levels are too high. The medical term for this is 'Hyperglycaemia'
- The blood Insulin levels are too low (Insulin helps to control blood glucose levels)
- In Diabetes Type 1 there is an absolute lack of effective Insulin, so those with this form of Diabetes are categorised as being 'Insulin dependent'. They need their Insulin from external sources and have daily injections of it.
- In Diabetes Type 2 there is not quite enough effective Insulin available in the body for the body's own needs. This maybe due to not enough being produced or to the mechanisms for blood sugar control being resistant to the action of Insulin.

A few years ago I came to the following synopsis or definition of Diabetes – to condense and simplify my understanding of the condition:

Another Look at Diabetes (25 July 2014)

Musing on Diabetes I wonder if there is a place for considering it as:

"A systemic, progressive arteriopathy characterised by an absolute, (in Diabetes Type 1 or Insulin-dependent Diabetes) or relative (in Diabetes Type 2) lack of effective insulin, as evidenced by sustained hyperglycaemia – see WHO criteria."

WHO criterion for Diabetes: a fasting plasma glucose level equal to or greater than 7.00 mmol per litre, or 126 mg/dL.

I wonder if Diabetes Type 1, Insulin Dependent Diabetes, may be due to the innocent consumption of the same foods found to be incompatible in Diabetes Type 2 which then leads to exhaustion of the body's ability to produce any effective Insulin.

The emotional landscape must also be corrected in all types of Diabetes.

The beauty of having the time and opportunity to see things from a different perspective and have such musings is another thing that enriches me. I feel so fortunate.

Suppressed emotions: any and many. Overall life has lost its sweetness.

DUODENAL ULCER

This, in my findings, is yet another result of food intolerance, exactly as with Irritable Bowel Syndrome. Again once the toxic foods are excluded completely, the medication associated with the condition can be withdrawn because the ulcer heals itself.

Hiatus Hernia and Acid Reflux usually disappear once the food intolerance package has been identified and the discipline to completely avoid these foods is well-established. Again the culprits are usually dairy products, often wheat, sometimes both; always refined sugar and often the terrible tetrad of coffee, chocolate, cola and cocoa.

A word of caution for those who hope that drinking decaffeinated coffee or decaffeinated tea will allow them to continue their habit. Very often the process of decaffeination is chemical and these chemical residues remain in the decaffeinated product. They too are unhealthy.

Furthermore, it is the coffee bean and the cocoa bean, which have many components other than caffeine, to which the client is sensitive. Hence the need to stop these completely.

Suppressed emotions: they find somethings are 'hard to swallow' (Hiatus Hernia) or 'can't stomach' something.

ECZEMA

In infants, Eczema is almost always due to dairy intolerance. Sometimes goat's milk is a suitable substitute to cow's milk.

FIBROIDS

I am aware that my findings on this are even further from the norm but bear with me. In my view it is evidence of the paucity of proper sex education and possibly an indictment of men. It relates to sexual intercourse.

During sex most men climax before their partner, so the men turn over, go to sleep while the woman is left high but I hope not dry. The energy has gone to the uterus stoking the climax which doesn't happen, leaving the energy stuck there. The energy flow is only completed when the woman too has her orgasm.

Without climax, that energy stays stuck in the womb where it stimulates the production of fibroids. These are tiny at first but grow as the woman's frustrations are repeated.

So ladies I would suggest that if/when you haven't climaxed you ensure that you do, either yourself or with your partner's help.

To me, the fibroids are evidence of recurrent sexual non-fulfilment.

The women I have suggested this hypothesis to have immediately agreed that this matches their experience. This confirmation has happened so often that I now accept it as cause and effect.

One curiosity: I think it was a Danish study on some aspect of sexual intercourse which found that those female participants who had kept their socks on climaxed earlier than those who were bare-foot. If you find it challenging to reach orgasm, who knows this simple ploy might be helpful. It's worth trying!

Suppressed emotions: feeling unloved, lonely, not treated as an equal.

GRIEF

The rupture in life that happens when someone you love dies, or a relationship dies, or there is any other deep loss, is permanent and painful. The duration of the pain is completely individual, as is its intensity.

In her book 'On Death and Dying', Elizabeth Kubler Ross described the stages that people go through in their journey through grief. These include denial, anger, bargaining and depression, before being able to reach a place of acceptance. The dwell-time in each stage is entirely individual and is also heavily influenced by the prevailing social, cultural, spiritual and philosophical norms.

The journey through grief needs to be completed otherwise the strong emotional energies (for example anger and resentment) stay stuck in the tissues and remain there, ultimately contributing to the generation of illness at a later stage.

To enable a route back to full health, the grieving person may need time on their own company as well as love and support from others. The key thing is that they are able to express their emotions and take the time they need to readjust and regain their equilibrium.

HEART ATTACK

This happens when an artery supplying blood to the heart muscle is blocked and the muscle beyond the blockage cannot receive the oxygen and nutrients essential for the survival of that muscle area which then dies. (See Arterial Disease).

Hyperbaric oxygen, cayenne pepper and intravenous Vitamin C may be useful – see under 'Stroke'

Suppressed emotions: sustained heartache, heartbreak, grief, feeling unloved.

KNOBBLY KNUCKLES NEXT TO THE NAILS, ALSO KNOWN AS 'HEBERDEN'S NODES'

These are lumpy bits on the last joints of fingers and thumbs. Often there are similar changes on the toes. They are typical of Osteoarthrosis (see later).

These are always associated with food intolerance; usually dairy products. These nodes reduce once the food exclusions are adhered to. Joint mobility increases and pain decreases.

HIGH BLOOD PRESSURE

The medical term is Hypertension or, most often, Idiopathic Hypertension. 'Idiopathic' simply means 'causes unknown'.

In my experience High Blood Pressure which falls into the Idiopathic category is caused by Food Intolerance; usually dairy products, refined sugar, often wheat. Caffeine is known to raise blood pressure and contribute to Cardiac Arrhythmias (irregular beats of the heart). Eliminating these toxins for 3 months will have an impact on the Blood Pressure. If this is favourable then these exclusions need to be lifelong. Very often the medication taken to control the Blood Pressure can be withdrawn after a while: it should be reduced as soon as the client notices dizziness, especially on rising from the lying to standing position.

Hyperbaric Oxygen may prove useful – See also Heart Attack and Stroke, Dementia.

IRRITABLE BOWEL SYNDROME (IBS)

This syndrome is a combination of all of the following symptoms: indigestion, heartburn, bloating, constipation, diarrhoea, bowel-urgency, aches and pains in bones and joints, inability to think straight, poor concentration. Again, the culprit is usually dairy products along with the tetrad of coffee, chocolate, cola, cocoa, plus refined sugar. Wheat may also cause a problem.

With IBS, the gut bacteria have typically been severely compromised, so taking a good quality probiotic to restore the gut microbiome will be vital to return the digestive system to full working order.

MENIERES DISEASE

A 60-year-old man who developed Meniere's Disease in 1992 had an Endo lymphatic shunt performed three years later. This gave him temporary respite from the Vertigo plus a myriad other symptoms, and permanent deafness in the right ear. His hearing had been normal pre-op.

I first saw him in July 2001. He still had, in his words, vertigo, dizziness, vomiting, tiredness, indigestion and phlegm from his lungs, and experienced them every other day.

Dealing with his whole health, I corrected his Brain Balance (Laterality), corrected the misalignments in his cervical spine using Osteopathy, and discerned his food intolerances.

He needed five treatment sessions with me before he fully detoxed and his symptoms totally disappeared.

On those five occasions I checked his Laterality and corrected it if necessary; checked his cervical spine and corrected if necessary and gave him Electronic Gem Therapy with Delta waves via emeralds and a green filter to his mastoid process to sedate the inner ear.

I find that Vertigo is over-activity in the inner ear, hence I sedate it.

May 2002 no Vertigo, no dizziness, no sickness, no tiredness, no indigestion, no phlegm.

Also in March 2002, an unexpected bonus: he no longer needed prisms in his spectacles for the first time in 30 years.

August 2002 to May 2006 he had no nausea or dizziness until, in that May, he inadvertently ate some cream in soup and felt miserable and cold and had dizzy turns lasting 5 to 30 seconds, accompanied by a lot of nausea.

In September 2014 I phoned him and asked if he still had any vertigo, dizziness, sickness, nausea, tiredness, indigestion or phlegm.

He said "No". The only thing he had was deafness in his right ear [which was Iatrogenic], apart from that he was feeling "very well."

Comment:

To me Vertigo/dizziness/Meniere's disease and Migraine are different expressions of the same problems, as long as space occupying lesions (brain tumours) have been ruled out.

Suppressed emotions: fear, insecurity.

MENTAL ILLNESS

The link between Gut/Heart/Brain has already been mentioned in the section titled 'Food Intolerance'. This link is, to me, fundamental in the development of mental illness. A brief reminder: the Vagus nerve has a controlling influence on the Gut, Heart and Brain. 90% of its fibres go from the Gut to the brain via the heart and other structures.

The ingestion of insecticides, pesticides, herbicides, antibiotics compromises the gut microbiome so proper gut function and nutritional absorption becomes abnormal.

I have yet to see anyone with a psychiatric condition who does not have food intolerances. My challenge: they simply don't believe it. Milk, sugar and caffeine seem the biggest culprits.

In anxiety the assemblage point is high on the right side of the chest, when this is near or above the collar bone the client is usually manic. The assemblage point is the centre of a client's energy field which, if healthy, is approximately the centre of the chest.

In depression the assemblage point is over the liver, the further it is downwards towards the navel the more depressed the person.

Thus in bi-polar illness, the assemblage point flips from high to low on the right side. In Schizophrenia it flips from the right side of the chest across to the left side when shifting between diverse emotional/mental states.

NB I read somewhere that 1 in 4 marijuana users between the ages of 17 and 24 become schizophrenic.

In my experience with addicts (Heroin, Cocaine and so) they usually started their journey with marijuana, so I am not convinced that the legalising of marijuana makes much sense.

There is no denying the presence of past emotional events being a trigger for mental illness yet long-term recovery cannot happen, in my experience, unless the food intolerances and microbiome are corrected.

My approach with mental illness is no different to the way I look at *all* illness.

- Identify all the toxins, physical, emotional and mental
- Select the enabling Bach Flower Remedies to balance their emotional/mental states and stimulate detoxing.
- Correct the laterality

- Correct the assemblage point, often with Electronic Gem therapy
- Check the vitamin and mineral levels. I find that people with mental health issues seem to have a peculiar propensity for being very short of Vitamin D3, often needing 10,000 units, 250 micrograms, daily for some months before reducing that to whatever maintenance dose is indicated
- Emphasise the central and utter importance of the need to *absolutely exclude* the toxic foods
- Keep their blood pH more alkaline with Barley Grass and a probiotic – the one I use has 12 happy bugs in it

After following this approach most clients who come back to see me remark on the greater mental and emotional stability they feel. Weights have lifted from their shoulders; they are joyous and laughing again.

'*In their own write*' has a contribution from someone who had long term depression.

MICROBIOME

When this is healthy, you are healthy. Everyone who is ill has an abnormal microbiome.

Honouring your food intolerances, loving yourself enough to stick to your exclusions, eating only organic foods where possible, avoiding WiFi, keeping your mobile phone in aeroplane mode (or switched off) when carrying it, are simple things you can do to maintain a healthy microbiome. Taking a good probiotic and something to keep your system alkaline e.g., barley grass, also enhances and supports a healthy microbiome, indeed your whole health.

MIGRAINE

Migraine and Vertigo are conditions in which I always find the 'Laterality' to be abnormal. Laterality refers to which hemisphere of the brain is dominant, and this is compromised by neck issues. More specifically, the cervical vertebrae are out of alignment. It is possible to test this and tell which side the migraine headache happens. To do this I have the client lying on their back on an examination couch. I feel their neck, aiming to locate the highest palpable lateral process, usually on the third cervical vertebra (third neck bone, counting from the top) to reveal an asymmetry, meaning one hand feels it, the other does not. The prominent side is the same side as the headache usually.

This is because the vertebral artery runs through canals in the top six cervical vertebrae. When one of these vertebrae is out of alignment with its neighbours, that artery becomes kinked and the blood flow therefore is reduced. I postulate that migraine happens when the brain demands more oxygen, therefore more blood flow is needed, and so other arteries expand to increase the needed blood supply. The pressure of that arterial expansion gives the typical migraine headache, often with the preceding aura indicating that the headache is on its way because the local blood supply is insufficient.

There are also food intolerances, usually to coffee, chocolate, cola, cocoa, along with dairy products.

Someone knocked on my door and asked if I remembered him. He said he had last seen me 35 years ago because of migraine and he hasn't had one since, but could I sort his neck out please!

MOTOR NEURONE DISEASE (SEE DEMENTIA)

MULTIPLE SCLEROSIS (SEE DEMENTIA)

NAUSEA IN PREGNANCY

The mother has most often had marked pregnancy nausea in the majority of infants with the symptoms of food intolerance. The mechanism is probably that the babe in the womb is reacting to the foods that Mum is innocently eating. If Mum was to stop these foods, it might well be seen that the pregnancy nausea subsides. A Swedish study in c1967 concluded that 65% of mums who had significant pregnancy nausea had babies who were food intolerant.

Somehow these valid observations have no current value; apparently such studies are considered (by the medical establishment) as being too old. In my view a truth is a truth, no matter how old it is.

It's important to be aware that mums with significant pregnancy nausea are highly likely to have a child with notable health issues, such as colic, constipation, diarrhoea, croup, eczema, asthma, repeated ear infections, recurrent sore throats. In later life these will lead to Diabetes, Juvenile Arthritis, Crohn's disease, Colitis, Rheumatoid and Hypertension.

The worst form of pregnancy nausea is Hyperemesis Gravidarum, which is severe vomiting in pregnancy. Would these mums benefit from excluding the most common food toxins, dairy, chocolate, coffees, cola, refined sugars and wheat? And do they also need to be watchful for their children having more food intolerance related conditions?

I also wonder whether Pre-Eclampsia in pregnancy might not have similar origins.

Breastfeeding mums may also find that by staying off these foods, they may avoid having colicky babies.

I don't know because I haven't tested anyone with Hyperemesis or Pre-Eclampsia but might they be worried sick?

OBESITY

In virtually every case, this is due to food intolerance. Again, it is usually dairy products, often wheat; the terrible tetrad of coffee, chocolate, cola, cocoa are almost always implicated as is refined sugar. On an emotional level, it can also be an unconscious form of protection.

Women of menstrual age tend to lose 1lb per week, but nothing in the premenstrual week. The weight loss continues for months/years until it finally stabilises.

Suppressed emotions: lack of self-worth, feeling unloved

OSTEOARTHROSIS

This is most always caused by food intolerance, unless there has been a preceding injury. In my experience osteoarthrosis is almost never 'wear and tear', unless there has been fracture either above or below the area of osteoarthrosis so leading to abnormal joint alignment and mechanics.

The culprit is usually milk, often wheat and occasionally both. Other foods that seem to be associated with osteoarthrosis include refined sugars, coffees, chocolate, cola, cocoa and alcohol.

Such clients usually have significant Heberden's Nodes (see Knobbly Knuckles Nearest the Nails, above).

An example: I saw a lady aged 85 with severe chronic osteoarthrosis whose right hand was a claw and had been for 3 years. She was completely unable to extend these fingers and was only able to hold a walking stick with a flat top. She had had seven surgeries to her feet, between 2001 and 2007, some successful, some not.

One year after she was first seen:

- she could completely extend and flex the fingers of her right hand
- she had lost 35lbs in weight
- she said she had "more energy than I've had in 50 years"
- she no longer needed an afternoon snooze
- her stamina was much increased
- her concentration and mental sharpness had returned
- her temperament was much more equable so her spells of apathy and depression had lifted

In a nutshell: her overall health was transformed.

I see this transformation repeatedly, but only in those who accept that the forbidden foods are toxic for them and in no sense constitute a 'treat'. When you think about it, how can something be thought of as a treat if it is damaging your health?

Suppressed emotions: anger, judgemental, dogmatic, inflexible.

OSTEOPOROSIS

Osteoporosis is the thinning of the bones which typically occurs in the elderly population.

Everyone focuses on Calcium when considering bone health, and of course it is important but it is not the only component. Other important components to bone health are Magnesium, Phosphorus and Boron.

Good sources of Magnesium are bananas, green leafy vegetables and a wide assortment of nuts, beans, seeds, fish, avocados, whole grains, yoghurt, dark chocolate. However, it is important to avoid the last two if dairy or cocoa intolerance are present.

Good sources of Phosphorus are all meats, most fish, lentils, beans, pumpkin seeds, sunflower seeds, grains.

Good sources of Boron are: avocados, beans, peas, legumes, nuts, broccoli, carrots, celery, onions, apples, bananas, oranges, pears, grapes, wine, beer, cider.

Why is Boron critical for bone health?

The parathyroid glands, which are four glands sitting in the back of the thyroid gland in the neck, have the biggest concentration of Boron of any tissue in the body. The parathyroid glands control bone health; the Chinese say that the Kidneys also control the bones. Therefore, it is always important to assess kidney function in those with Osteoporosis.

Boron tablets are available widely and typical dose is one 3mg tablet three times daily.

A word about Calcium in milk: I heard of an elderly cheesemaker who said that the Calcium in milk is no longer available nutritionally because of the processing of the milk. Apparently the large coffee house chains ask that the milk is heated to even higher temperature so that they can produce lattes with long-lasting froth. This further heating apparently denatures the Casein, a protein in the milk, to the point where it forms an impenetrable barrier around the Calcium in the milk. This renders the Calcium unavailable to the body's metabolism.

Therefore, the price of a good latte is apparently to turn milk into a simple white fluid with little nutritional value, especially in terms of Calcium availability.

Vitamin D3 and K2 are also essential for good bone health. These levels need to be assessed, supplemented and monitored.

It is also essential that the gut microbiome is healthy, and adequately supplemented with good probiotics; this enables the easy absorption of all minerals, vitamins and components essential for the health of all tissues and organs in the body, including the bones.

Regular and routine exercise is also of significant benefit.

A word about conventional treatments for Osteoporosis. Calcium tablets are poorly absorbed. The Biphosphonates are compounds given orally, or by injection, to people with Osteoporosis. These compounds produce an apparent improvement when assessed by x-ray. There is only one problem: they harden the external surface of the bones, which looks good on x-ray, yet they cause what an engineer would understand as brittle fracture when the client falls, breaking that bone.

Bones, surprisingly, have a degree of flex and 'give'. The surface hardening due to the Biphosphonates robs the bones of this flex and the fracture usually occurs in the surface-hardened area of the bone.

So Biphosphonates are only *apparently* effective when bones are assessed by x-ray; they are also expensive, given by injection, and have multiple side-effects.

Boron is much cheaper, much simpler, is taken orally and has very few (if any!) unwanted effects.

PAIN AND THE EFFECTS OF MENTAL AND EMOTIONAL PAIN

Pain makes each of us selfish as it is almost impossible to ignore. Physical pain if severe makes us scream with anguish; if intolerable makes us ghostly quiet, unless someone tries to move us.

Emotional pain is exactly the same.

We cry and scream and shout so that all know our emotional distress. But intolerable emotional pain makes us withdraw. We become quiet, introspective, detached from ordinary life. The magnitude of the pain reflects in our level of detachment, withdrawal. We internalise the hurt completely. The greater the hurt, the greater the withdrawal. The withdrawal can express as syncope that is fainting or, if massively extreme, in death from coronary spasm; literally heart-break.

Mental pain is equivalent to emotional pain. Worries such as overthinking, can give the physical symptoms of anxiety as in can't settle, can't concentrate, distant look in eyes. Torrential thoughts lead to mental shutdown, equivalent to syncope, which is fainting; switch-off. Complete withdrawal.

We are desperately frightened when in severe pain, we need to feel safe, loved, cared for and the pain to be properly managed for the reassurance to flow.

PERIODS

Pre-Menstrual Tension is made much, much worse by eating chocolate, coffee, coca, cola – sorry! If you can avoid the temptation, I can assure you it will be worth it. Painful periods [Dysmennorrhoea] is also associated with chocolate, coffee, cola, cocoa, and often dairy products.

One further curiosity about coffee: sometimes I can test someone's reaction to chocolate and there may be no response, in other words the body might be able to take it; yet if I then test for coffee and they react to that then I return to check them against chocolate they now react to the chocolate. So coffee seems to have a sensitising relationship with chocolate. This may also be true of the other caffeine-containing compounds like cola. This is why stopping coffee, chocolate, cola and cocoa together avoids this mutual sensitisation.

Once these foods have been stopped, two things happen:

- their next period is heavier than normal
- that next period arrives unexpectedly because there are no warning symptoms, no menstrual cramps or PMT, so I warn them to be prepared to be surprised.

Thereafter the flow is lighter, much more normal and lives can continue with much more equanimity than before.

The exception is those with heavy periods (Mennorrhagia); this is the only group when the first period after their total food exclusions is lighter than they have recently experienced.

This may seem a bit odd to be included here yet, when I hear that the female keeper at a zoo has been mauled by one of the big cats under her care, I always wonder if the keeper was menstruating at the time. Those animals can smell blood from a great distance. I guess their natural reflex is to consider that the source of the blood is an injured animal which would be easy prey.

PILES (HAEMORRHOIDS)

The chief mechanic of the Andy Rouse Motor Racing team gave me this tip (I was their honorary medical officer for a few years). He said that Ground Elder (Bishopweed) is good for piles, whether in pregnancy (after the first 3 months) or in later life. You chew the about 2 inches (5cm) of the stem of the plant 3 or 4 times a day. Ensure there is no herbicide or pesticide or similar on the plant. Discard the stem once it has been well chewed.

I have offered this tip to several clients who all attest to its usefulness.

RHEUMATOID ARTHRITIS

Rheumatoid is always associated with food intolerance; usually dairy products, often wheat, occasionally both. I also advise that they cut their caffeine and sugar intake. In most cases they need to stop all of these foods completely in order to heal.

One feature of those with Rheumatoid is how long and how painful the detoxing period can be once these foods have been stopped. It can go on as long as 12-16 weeks or more, and be so severe that the patient can no longer endure the pain and so revert to their former diet. This is truly unfortunate because if they really wish to reverse their Rheumatoid, they have to go through this detoxing period from the beginning again.

Suppressed emotions: anger, resentment, judgmental, dogmatic, inflexible.

SINUSITIS (CHRONIC)

This is usually due to dairy intolerance and not infection. The giveaway is the colour of the lining of the nose. When infection is the source of the Sinusitis, the nasal mucosa (the lining of the nose) is a bright carmine red colour; when allergy/food intolerance is the cause then this lining is a silvery grey, almost blueish hue.

STROKES

A stroke is either a bleed into the brain or a clot in an artery supplying blood to some part of the brain. In either case the brain tissue beyond that bleed or clot cannot get blood and therefore oxygen and nutrients and so dies. That means that area of brain cannot function, so impaired speech and mobility can result, as can death.

To my mind Hyperbaric Oxygen would get as much Oxygen into the brain tissue as possible and so limit the amount of damage and impairment.

The production of free radicals could be reduced by intravenous Vitamin C or, preferably, sodium ascorbate.

Cayenne pepper has a long history of usefulness in Herbal Medicine. Giving Cayenne pepper at the first onset of Stroke or heart attack needs also to be studied.

NB It is quite likely that no drug company would sponsor such research and would probably threaten to withdraw all research funding from any university contemplating such work.

TIREDNESS

Tiredness is an indication that the body does not have enough energy to support the current demands being made of it. That fatigue will also have a powerful emotional component. The mental 'noise' may reflect an unwillingness to want to participate in what is currently happening, and a lack of volition permeates the physical body and demands that it switch off, take good long rest, recover and then resume normal life.

The power of emotions to influence body energy should never be underestimated. Consider the Oxford / Cambridge Boat Race. Sixteen of the fittest guys on the planet are in two teams of eight and they row from Putney to Mortlake on the River Thames. They have trained incredibly hard for almost a year.

At the end of the race, the victorious team look like they would happily do it all over again; the other team hardly has the energy between them to lick a stamp. The difference? Winning and losing, and the accompanying emotion.

The exhilaration, the excitement, the ecstasy of winning permeates one crew totally; the despair, the shame, the unimaginable devastation felt by the losers drains their energy completely. All that anticipation shattered. That illustrates the power of emotions to affect the physical bodies.

Physically the body can do far, far more than most people can imagine. In extreme athletic events, for example the Marathons de Sables (a 250km race across the desert), it is the mental toughness that carries the competitors through to complete the event. Once doubt or uncertainty enters the mind there can only be one of two outcomes: the mind dismisses the uncertainty completely and the participant continues, or the niggle grows, the determination erodes, eventually leading to withdrawal from the race, either from an injury or fatigue.

My assumption is always that the inability to deal with doubt initiates the withdrawal from a race, whatever the nature of that exit may appear to be on the surface.

Mental resilience determines physical stamina. The Armed Forces know this, the best examples being the Special Forces. Mental resilience decays in the presence of persisting negative emotional input.

Ulcerative Colitis

I have always found this to be related to coffees, cola, cocoa, chocolate, caffeine itself therefore to include tea; plus beef, milk and all its products, and very often wheat as well.

Suppressed emotions: anger, conflict, fear, grief, rage, shame, terror.

Vaccination

Vaccination is considered to be part of prevention in Medicine.

Before delving into this in more detail please bear in mind that Medicine prides itself that best practice is always applied because it is evidence based and the gold standard for this evidence is the randomly controlled trial.

As far as I am aware the vaccination programmes for infants and children have *never* been subject to randomly controlled trials, therefore there is no objective academic evidence that these are effective. That evidence base is assumed, taken for granted, although there is no dispassionate data to reinforce that stance. In a court of law it would be treated as hearsay and therefore be inadmissible.

Such a study would mean that a group of people would be randomly allocated to being a Test or Control subject. Ideally neither they nor the assessors of the trial would know whether they had the full vaccine or had just been given the carrier material.

Monitoring the Test group over the next few years would determine exactly how effective a vaccine is and what complications might arise from the full vaccine. Following the Control group would reveal any side-effects from the carrier material used.

It is my view that randomly controlled trials are *essential* before any vaccination programme can be offered to the public.

There is a complicating factor.

In the 1980s pharmaceutical companies were concerned about their potential bankruptcy due to the amount of litigation arising from vaccine injury damage claims. Some American companies threatened to close their facilities and stop the manufacture of vaccines altogether. They pointed out to the Government that if all these facilities were closed then there would be no resources for the government to call upon in the event of a biological warfare attack. The government agreed that the vaccine manufacturers were no longer liable for vaccine injury claims which then became a government responsibility.

Consequently the manufacturers of the vaccine cannot be blamed or financially penalised for injuries due to vaccination.

Is that fair? Is that morally acceptable? Is it just?

As medical students we were taught that the effectiveness of vaccination was a given. Objectively this blind, uncritical acceptance has no place in any discipline.

The only answer is randomly controlled trials which are carried out *without* any drug company involvement i.e. such a study is outwith the influence of any group with a commercial vested interest in the outcome.

Here's a paradox.

In vaccination a tiny dose of the organism is given in the hope of provoking an immune response so that those who have been vaccinated have nothing to fear from a big dose of that same organism. The principle of vaccination is that *like cures like*. This is the homeopathic principle and it is being used in conventional medicine! This leads me to these thoughts:

- if the vaccine was pure i.e. without added extras then that is the vaccine that should be tested in one randomly controlled trial
- the vaccine with the added extras should be the subject of another randomly controlled trial.
- a homeopathic equivalent e.g. Morbillinum against measles should be studied, again in a randomly controlled trial.

Monitoring the outcomes in each group over the next decades would give factual scientific hard data on the relative merits and side-effects of all the vaccine types tested. The cost per dose should also be assessed.

The end point of these studies should clearly reveal:

- The number of cases of influenza in the vaccinated and unvaccinated populations
- The number of cases of Measles, Mumps, Rubella in the vaccinated and unvaccinated populations
- The number of cases of illness x in the vaccinated and non-vaccinated groups
- The complications arising in each group both short-medium- and long-term (10-20 years)

Only when all these data are analysed objectively without commercial influence can the true costs, complications and benefits of any vaccination programme be truly known.

How do vaccine producers explain the outbreak of measles in a College residence in which 100% of the students had been vaccinated?

Once these data are validated and become available then the true effectiveness of any vaccination programme can be rigorously concluded.

The public is then able to make an *informed* decision about whether to present their child or themselves for vaccination without influence from those with a commercial interest, who will always put a spin on the value of their product, and try persuasion through generating fear within those citizens.

VERTIGO (SEE ALSO MENIERE'S DISEASE)

I think that Vertigo is overactivity of the balance system in the inner ear and a response to the diminished blood flow through the vertebral arteries, for the same reason that arterial kinking contributes to Migraine.

I treat Vertigo by:

Re-aligning the neck bones, identifying any contributory food intolerances then cooling the energy in the Labyrinth using Electronic Gem Therapy with Delta waves through emeralds and a green filter.

A client's story is given under Meniere's Disease.

THEORETICAL MEDICINE

There are departments of Theoretical Physics and Theoretical Maths, why not Departments of Theoretical Medicine? Why not spark original thinking with the aim of generating more effective approaches in Medicine? Given that this is one of my passions, I have captured the essence of my thinking on a number of subjects. It is my hope that it stimulates debate and possibly moves things in a new and ever more helpful and healing direction. I fully accept that there may already be, and have been, research into such more effective approaches of which I am completely unaware in these fields. I hope that is so.

Plainly such a department must be set up *without* any vested financial interest from any external source so that the research can be truly independent of commercial involvement. Many philanthropists have mountains of money which they would love to see used in a way which truly has the benefit of humanity at heart.

COMA

Might the normal, healthy electrical polarity of the head be reversed in those in a Coma?

In the book 'The Body Electric' by Becker, R O, and Selden, G, published by Harper Collins in New York in 1985, on page 116, they write: 'it [the normal electrical polarity of the brain] is reversed in direction in both normal sleep and anaesthesia'. Coma mimics normal sleep and has many of the features of being anaesthetised.

Might restoring the normal polarity of the brain hasten recovery from Coma?

Which prompts a further question:

Can the need for anaesthetics be reduced by reversing the polarity of the conscious brain?

HEART ATTACK AND STROKE

These are caused when an artery is blocked or leaks. This leakage or blockage stops the heart muscle or brain tissue beyond that point from receiving enough Oxygen and nutrients. That tissue then dies. The more tissue that is damaged the more disability in function results, sometimes leading to death of the person.

Saturating the tissue with Oxygen would reduce the tissue damage. This can be done with Hyperbaric Oxygen which provides the gas at pressure above normal ambient pressure.

I wonder if, in future, there might be flying squads of Hyperbaric chambers with staff trained to put in intravenous ascorbate going to households where there is someone with either suspected stroke or heart attack, so beginning the treatment in the ambulance before the person gets to hospital.

Any production of Reactive Oxygen Species (ROS) can be neutralised by giving intravenous Sodium Ascorbate during the Hyperbaric treatment.

ORGAN TRANSPLANT

Is it possible to build a bank of tissue for transplantation?

Is there some way to render tissue for transplantation non-antigenic and keep it in a healthy nutritional medium with Oxygen bubbled through it?

Then such a tissue bank can be established and the drama and haste removed from tissue transplantation.

Plus the patient will not need to keep taking drugs to suppress their immune system to reduce the risk of rejection of the transplanted tissue over the rest of their lives.

HARNESSING COMPUTING POWER

Following people through life from the point of conception to the point of death and noting their illness experience along the way would give huge amounts of data and at last enable linkages between life events and disease to be identified.

Questions such as:

- Which environmental impacts most affect which disease state or illness generation?
- Which occupational factors influence illness development in what ways?
- Is there a link between planetary phases and illness/accident?
- Is there an incontrovertible link between birth-sign (which is actually a reflection of the date of conception) and illness?
- Do those who have been vaccinated have more illness than those not? For example more medical consultations, more time off school, more infections, more leukaemia, more cancer than the unvaccinated population?

A myriad of these and other epidemiological questions could be answered, to everyone's benefit given that such longterm data could be gathered and analysed.

STEM CELLS

These are cells which are the precursor to all types of cell in the body. They have the potential to become any type of cell and are part of the body's tissue repair mechanism.

Bruce Lipton in his book 'The Biology of Belief' describes how he cultured stem cells with identical DNA yet which produced three different types of tissue. This led him to progress the theory that it cannot be the DNA which controls the cell but the environment in which that cell exists. This environment informs the cell membrane which then instructs the DNA. He calls the cell membrane the 'brain' ('brane') of the cell.

Apparently there are six populations of stem cell in the human body (if my memory serves). Stem cells will become a major part of treatments for tissue repair in the future, yet I have a concern. The environment controlled the outcome in Lipton's three cell cultures. When stem cells are inserted they will probably develop according to the prevailing conditions around them. If those surroundings are full of toxins then they will likely eventually produce tissue resembling the diseased tissue they are aimed at correcting and the treatment will be deemed a failure. That would, at least in theory, be inevitable – unless the milieu external to those cells is detoxed first of all.

In summary my theory is that stem cells can successfully replicate and repair diseased or damaged tissue only if the ecology of the local terrain is restored to its natural healthy state.

IN THEIR OWN WRITE

These testimonials are the stories of some of my clients in their own words and with their permission.

[NB. Anything in italics and square brackets is added by the author for clarification or a wee bit more information. Otherwise, the writing is exactly as it was received.] All names have been changed out of respect for confidentiality.

.oOo.

Dear Roger

Although I wanted to write this card for you, finding words adequate to describe my thanks and gratitude are impossible. This goes far beyond concept and idea.

My gratitude is more than personal. It's gratitude for having a being who has made an unshifting, imperturbable commitment to healing and (it seems to me) has spent his life dedicated to this.

On a personal level I'm sure you have a sense of what this has meant to me but thank you from the deepest heart space, not only on this occasion but from more than 30 years ago for the healing my daughter *[then aged 2]* received.

My wish is for your long life and well-being and the continuation of the blessings you bring to others.

Much love,

C D

A CASE OF SEVERE CONSTIPATION

[Written by the child's mother]

By the time *['Dan']* was 2½ he had seen over 40 health professionals I had taken him to, within the NHS and privately. Since he was born his bowel habits had been odd, severe diarrhoea as a breastfed baby, then once weaned, severe constipation that could only be controlled with copious doses morning and night of Senokot and Lactulose. He was in constant pain, frightened to go to the toilet, could not be potty trained and was anxious and distressed all the time, his behaviour was becoming a real problem and they were talking of psychological intervention. He was underweight and height, pale and undernourished as any food he ate ran right through him because of the medication... I was labelled an 'overanxious mother' and was even asked to leave a doctor's surgery practice list because I pestered them so much to find out 'WHY' is he constipated, please find a reason why, don't just tell me it's just because and send us weekly to a constipation clinic for monitoring.

Then I was referred by a client of mine to Roger. That day I had driven many miles with a screaming toddler [*3 years old*] in the back seat, my [*new*] car broke down on the way, I was late and the prospect of spending another amount of money – I had spent hundreds of pounds – 'trying to find the answer', was weighing heavily on me. When Roger answered the door I could have cried, he guided us to his room got us both at ease and within an hour had diagnosed a severe dairy allergy, gave *[him]* some 'magic drops' and sent us on our way to a dairy free life. My fear confirmed, yet I had not had the confidence to remove milk from my son's diet as all the other doctors had said that it was ridiculous to suggest such a thing! We left there, I entered [*emptied*] every cupboard of foodstuff from our home that contained any milk products, (with everyone around me telling me I was mad!) And shopping for anything I could find was 'safe' for *[him]* to eat. Within 3 days the difference was just unbelievable – I was able to remove all medication and *[he]* was able to go to the toilet like a normal child, within a week he was fully potty trained and the happiest little boy in the world. Yes it was sometimes difficult to eat out, birthdays et cetera but *[he]* was so good even as a young child, he knew if he was even to take a tiny amount of dairy product in any form he would be ill again – he never once veered off that path. On our final visit to the 'constipation clinic' I met the Senior consultant *[actually the Professor of Paediatrics.]* and as you can imagine I was very vocal on the situation that I felt I had been left in and how difficult it had been – I wanted answers as to why they had never tested him and brushed me off when I had even suggested it. He said "they don't always get it right and there was no money to investigate other alternative options" he later sent me a personal apology by letter.

Dan remained dairy free until only recently – he's big strong healthy 15-year-old now and he decided to try and eat a Malteser chocolate and when there were no ill effects gradually introduced dairy – he can now eat anything at all, although anything very creamy or cheesy is not to his taste which is no bad thing... He still will only eat small amounts of chocolate, but has a freedom he never thought he would have. Dan still talks of Roger 'saving him' and I wholeheartedly agree. I often reflect on how different our lives would have been had we not got the proper diagnosis and we will both be eternally grateful to Roger.

[Dan realises now that his milk and milk products exclusion is lifelong because at the age of 20 he had a duodenal ulcer, which I find is another symptom of milk

intolerance. He is currently on no medication, is absolutely symptom-free and is thriving].

MY DAMASCENE MOMENT

I first consulted Dr Roger Melhuish about 1984 when I was 50. At the time I was having trouble with parasites which the NHS consultant gastroenterologist was not taking seriously. A friend recommended Dr Melhuish and I made an appointment. After the consultation he prescribed a powder to be taken in a glass of brandy. A Dr from heaven! I thought this is my kind of Dr. This was the start of a difficult journey that changed my life and brought me peace 35 years later at the age of 85. Dr Melhuish's aim was to treat the causes of illness and not the effects. I had been affected by severe negativity all my life with an underlying deep depression which manifested as many illnesses: frequent bronchitis, fluey colds, ear infections, styes in childhood, and in later life, diverticulitis, arthritis, frequent influenza, duodenal ulcer, auto-immune disease, osteoporosis and acid reflux. I knew I wanted to be well but didn't know how. Over the years Dr Melhuish gave me direction and sign-postings to courses, books and temporary diets some of which, along with various treatments including gem therapy, acupuncture, homeopathic and vibrational drops taken internally and other therapies, changed my negative thinking and guided me to better health. I know that without his help I would have been dead long ago.

My feelings, thoughts and actions were not acceptable to my mother. My mother was very skilled in administering the emotional solar plexus punch when least expected. My "go to" method of coping with my mother from early childhood and so with stress was to withdraw and suppress all emotion. Thus in order to survive alongside my mother I became an emotionless dutiful robot. I had no sense of self therefore no self-confidence, nor had I any boundaries. There was no room in my mother's life for me other than a chattel who could do well and enhance my mother's persona. I got by because I was very capable and people thought I was confident. I was head girl at school. Actually I was a nothing.

LOOKING BACK

I always froze in my mother's company but it never dawned on me that I could do anything about it. I didn't realise I was always unhappy because that's how it had always been and my mother was always telling me how happy I was. The only way I could escape from her was through learning and academic study which was a great solace to me. Nobody could invade my privacy when I was learning. I went to university expected to gain an honours degree. I received only an ordinary degree. Later, I realised I was so emotionally stunted and immature there had been no hope of an honours degree. I married, had 4 children, followed by a nervous breakdown. I was so withdrawn I could hardly walk or speak. I would only go into hospital on the condition that my mother would not be allowed to visit. I knew she was a problem but couldn't see in what way nor how to deal with it. I remember the psychiatrist asking me if I'd ever had a traumatic experience. I replied without thinking, "Living with my mother is a traumatic experience". I had no idea that there was anything I could do about that because that was how it had been since birth. I dutifully brought up the children in an emotionless state with no love. With the result they all have issues but are all wonderful and very supportive to their parents in old age. Later in life I realised I was in my mother's thrall and am amazed I never thought of leaving home as soon as I was earning. I was always physically tired with no energy and everything was an effort but it never occurred to me that I could do anything about it. PTSD?

I worked as a teacher until the children arrived. I ran a girl guide company in my fifties. I did other voluntary work all my life. When I was 66 I became ill with a severe auto-immune disease, could find no help to cope with the condition, set up a support group in 2005 and the first charity in the UK specifically for the condition in 2008. I ran this charity for 7 years with the help of a few volunteers while still ill. Under two Chairpersons it has developed beyond my wildest dreams. All this time there were many illnesses rearing their ugly heads because of all the negative gunge I had accumulated over the years.

LOOKING FORWARD

When I was 85 I went on a fortnight's retreat, on my own, armed with 3 self-help books, another 3 on my kindle and Dr Google. My mother had sucked the life out of me since birth and I became this emotionless dutiful robot and in later life felt I had died so that she could live. On my retreat I realised she had been an "energy vampire". Her friends used to say to me in my teens, "Of course, your mother is one of these people who lives off other people's energy". It never occurred to me that I was one who provided this energy nor did it dawn on me that I could do anything about it. Then, what did I do? I married an "energy vampire". All my life I thought I was in this world for the convenience of other people. I never considered that I had any rights or boundaries, nor had I any sense of self, so I was open to any " energy vampires" who came along. On my retreat I learned how to cope with an "energy vampire" and I now have energy, stamina and joy in my life. I don't remember ever having felt joy before.

I do believe that all illness is caused by negative thinking (which can be inherited) and, by dealing with negativity, illness can be resolved. I never felt rooted. Now I feel well and truly rooted and I like the feeling. I've worked hard to reach this point by changing my thinking but without the guidance of Dr Roger Melhuish I would have got nowhere. I was so lucky to find 'my kind of Dr' who led and directed me along a path which dealt with my many issues, finally resolving them and creating good health. My strength and stamina have returned. Nothing is an effort now. I have inner peace, joy, good health and freedom now that I have been released from a prison sentence of 85 years. I have finally learned to love. I am so very grateful. How many people are given the chance to improve their life at 85?

A BRAIN TUMOUR IN A 21-YEAR-OLD

My daughter [RW] was diagnosed with progressive neurological symptoms and a MRI scan carried out on 28 January 2020 confirmed she had a tumour in the area of the brain, which will was later diagnosed as a brainstem glioma -an aggressive intrinsic brain tumour. She was admitted to hospital and started on a course of Radiotherapy treatment on 6 February 2020.

During the first week of her radiotherapy treatment her speech, mobility and swallowing ability deteriorated rapidly and the following week it was clear her condition was getting worse. On the recommendation of a friend, and after 8th DXT radiotherapy treatment didn't improve her condition I contacted Doctor Roger Melhuish and made an appointment for [my daughter] to see him [on 15th February] as an outpatient. I had to take her in a wheelchair for her appointment as she was unable to walk and Roger and I had to help her into the surgery as the strength in her legs and her coordination were extremely poor and she was unable to speak and had to use a voice aid computer to make herself understood.

[Her coordination and power were so compromised that she had difficulty in locating and pressing the right button on this voice aid].

She started having Gem Beam Vibration Treatment and Roger also prescribed his Salvestrol tablets. After treatment Roger made up a specific blend of natural drops to help with her emotional well-being. *RW* tells me when she gets her treatment she sits on a chair which is a Multi-Wave Oscillator with Rife tube and feels a buzzing energy flowing through her body. When she had her first vibration treatment she was able to eat a burger, which we find amazing, as before that she had been unable to eat solid food and had struggled to swallow.

[Next appointment 28th February: Seeing her walk from the car supported by her Dad and climbing the few steps into the house brought tears to my eyes].

After *[this]* her second session she was able to tie her shoelaces, which she had previously been unable to do as her coordination was very poor. *[She]* feels great after every treatment and believes Roger is a miracle medicine man. We both love Roger as we have noticed a significant improvement in her condition since starting her treatment. On twentieth February she was able to walk again, with the aid of a walking frame. Her speech has slowly improved and she is now able to eat and swallow food normally. She was released from hospital on 28 February 2020.

[At her appointment on 9th April 2020: Told me she goes jogging].

[*She*] has finished her radiotherapy treatment but has continued with the vibration treatment and is still taking the tablets and drops because they make her feel so much better. She has had her three-month MRI scan on 1 June and we were told that her tumour had shrunk. Her next MRI scan is in 6 months time and we are hopeful the result will be positive.

Although[*she*] finished her course of radiotherapy at the hospital it was only when she started taking the Salvestrol tablets and drops and having her vibration treatment that we noticed an improvement in her condition, as up to then she was rapidly deteriorating. I strongly believe the vibration treatment and Salvestrol tablets and drops have saved my daughter's life and I would recommend this treatment to others. I know my daughter feels the same way.

Signed MM *[Father]* / RW *[Daughter]*

[Date received 17/07/20]

MY AF/HOMEOPATHY JOURNEY

Was diagnosed with paroxysmal atrial fibrillation in January 2019 having had many heart episodes in previous years but eventually got a diagnosis. I started on the appropriate medications but was finding that my quality of life and emotional outlook was hugely affected by the uncertainty of the condition. I was very anxious and was worried about when the next attack might be. The attacks could happen at any time and could last for many hours and I was always exhausted after such an attack. My anxiety was also heightened hugely throughout the attack. The stroke risk during an attack was also explained clearly to me. There was an option last year that I could also add another and the arrhythmia pill to my medication list. This I have not done. I have continued to take my prescription drugs throughout the homeopathic treatment.

I saw Doctor Melhuish on 20/11/2019

Symptoms before homeopathic treatment started:

- Paroxysmal atrial fibrillation
- Light-headedness and dizziness
- Indigestion
- Ectopic heartbeats
- Anxiety and fear of an attack / anxiety about staying away from home and travel
- Joint pain in feet

Effect of taking homeopathic drops

- Reduced AF attack number (1 attack on 6/12/19 lasting 4 hours and a recent attack lasting 7 hours on 14/06/20) *[a consequence of great distress re: very close friend who was critically ill]*
- Almost no light-headedness and dizziness
- Almost no indigestion
- Less ectopic heartbeats although some old beats and flutters
- Less fearful and less anxiety and increased confidence
- Still joint pain in feet
- Weight loss 3 kg
- Healthier bowel

Doctor Melhuish sees the patient as a whole and unique person. I believe my AF and other symptoms were due to increased inflammation in my body. Doctor M has been very supportive and I have phoned him on a couple occasions in the early days of taking the drops as I was unsure and anxious about the detoxing symptoms that I was experiencing. These can be alarming but an essential part of the healing process. My advice is to please be patient and allow this healing process to take place. I am hopeful that this recent AF attack can be sorted by the next set drops and all will be well. I would have come back to see Doctor Melhuish sooner. Covid has delayed my return visit by several months.

Homeopathy has helped me physically and emotionally and I would recommend this as a real and effective option.

Thank you Doctor Melhuish

P.M.

*[NB the 'Homeopathy' that this lady refers to is actually Vibrational medicine in that it is the specific mix of frequencies that **she** needs].*

[She also remarked: "You are the only one who has connected all the dots."]

A CASE OF CHEMICAL POISONING

Previous to the pesticide exposure I was extremely healthy and fit (University of Dundee Physiology Department assessment – about the level of an Olympic athlete).

At the time I was Principal Teacher of Biology at *[named]* High School.

After the summer holidays in 1999, there were complaints from staff and pupils of being bitten by "fleas" in two classrooms in the terrapin hut. This persisted over several weeks, so on the morning of Wednesday 15th September, the local authority was informed and classes relocated to other classrooms.

The local authority said they were unable to action the complaint until the middle of the following week. Staff was informed.

However, after lunch on the same day (15/09/1999), I entered one of the affected classrooms to collect the books and equipment for the 1st year class, to take to the relocated classroom. No pupil entered the room.

I noticed all the surfaces, floors and desks et cetera were wet, but I assumed the janitor had used the opportunity of the empty classroom to clean everything. There were no warning notices. During the subsequent lesson, I experienced extreme discomfort, burning eyes, throat, rapid heartbeat and chest pains, and loss of voice. The learning support teacher who was present in the room, noticed my distress and brought me a glass of water. To avoid alarming the pupils I continued the lesson.

At the end of the lesson, I returned the pupils' books and equipment back to the original classroom. No pupil assisted me, so no one else came into the classroom.

While there, the janitor entered the room and "reprimanded" me for being in the room, as it had been treated with pesticide and was to be kept isolated for a week. (There were no notices – what about the Health and Safety and COOSH regulations?)

I had a very disturbed night and the following morning, Thursday, I went to see my G P. There was no signs of infection, though my throat was inflamed. I had lost my voice and felt drained of energy. I was advised to rest and avoid aggravating my throat by not going to a swimming pool, and to return after the weekend if my condition hadn't improved.

On the Monday, I returned to the doctors, and though the inflammation in the throat was reduced, nor still any sign of infection, my energy levels had deteriorated.

I needed to sleep for many hours after any even light activity.

I developed digestion problems, as my body reacted badly to some foods.

I found it extremely difficult to keep warm; my waist, hips, legs and feet were cold to touch.

I had pressure headaches.

My eyesight and memory were affected and weak.

Coordination was impaired.

These conditions continued.

I had weekly reviews with the GP, though she was frustrated that she was unable to help, except to advise rest.

I attempted to return to work after 4 weeks, but was so completely exhausted by lunchtime, I was a hazard in a science classroom.

After persistent and repeated requests I was eventually informed (17/11/1999) by the school (not the local authority) with the name of the chemical used; a permethrin based compound that was widely used and considered safe for use in schools, and nits in children's hair. (But banned in the EU on 13/06/2000).

During the following months my health did not improve, and my body started to emit a horrible smell of rotten or decomposing meat/flesh.

During this period I actively sought alternative methods of healing; herbal medicine, homeopathy, naturopathic, as my GP was unable to help, except once to prescribe antidepressants, which had a disastrous effect on my already low energy levels.

In February 2000, I had a medical assessment for sickness benefit. I failed, and was informed by the doctor *"Nothing was wrong with me that a good kick up the backside wouldn't cure"*.

I was really angry with this diagnosis. I considered it flawed but felt helpless to challenge it. So, I contacted the

Pesticide Trust in London for a list of doctors who had experience in treating people exposed to pesticides.

On the list supplied was a medical doctor who lived about 10 miles away: Dr Roger Melhuish, Newburgh, Fife.

I telephoned Dr Melhuish , who said he could see me, provided I bring a sample of water, and a written summary of: (1) my current symptoms, (2) my medical history, and (3) the medical history of my parents and siblings.

Initially I thought the "sample of water" was a urine sample, it was to be a sample of my drinking water; *"very strange"* I thought.

The following week I visited Dr Melhuish at his consulting rooms in Newburgh.

On entering the consulting room, I was confused as there was no examination table visible.

All my previous medical examinations had involved physical examinations; blood pressure, breathing and heart stethoscope investigations et cetera.

Dr Melhuish asked me to sit in a chair beside the desk, asked if I had brought the written summary of my medical history, which he took and without even glancing at it, immediately turned it over and ignored. Then said *"We'll see what you have missed out later!"*. I was not amused; all that time spent on it, just to be ignored!

He then placed the jar of drinking water on a small platform and asked me to hold a metal baton. The baton was connected by a lead to the platform and a galvanometer meter, which was also connected to a probe which he tapped on the nail bed of my little finger; to form a circuit.

The meter registered a reading and a high-pitched whine; to be followed by Dr Melhuish saying *"You can't drink that water!"*

I replied: "It's my tapwater. What am I going to drink?"

In a dismissive and offhanded way he said: "I don't know, but you can't drink **that** water."

I was really confused and upset: no physical examination, disregarding all the work of complying my medical history, and now telling me I couldn't drink my tap water because of the whine and reading on a galvanometer! What was going on? My hopes were in shatters.

He then proceeded for the next 40 minutes tapping my little finger with the probe, while consulting a folder with lists of blue writing, occasionally placing phials of liquid or crystals on the platform of the machine, during which the machine gave out high-pitched whines of different frequencies and the needle on the meter flicked back and forth.

Dr Melhuish made notes during this "process", but my questions about what was happening were rebutted with a concentrated silence. Except for one interlude, when he gave me a yellow post-it with the words magnesium, selenium, and vitamins C written on it, and the instruction: "*You need to take these.*"

This was the only interaction!

At the end of the 40 minutes, I was boiling inside with anger and frustration about this waste of time, and with the loss of my expectations/hopes.

And "he" had the gall to charge for this, when the illness was creating so many financial problems. It was not fair!

Then Dr Melhuish read out his notes. He detailed all my symptoms, describe my condition and gave a detailed account of critical chemical levels in my body, my medical history, a list of foods that were not supportive or beneficial to my health, and emotional and mental factors in my life.

He also informed me of conditions that I, and my siblings, had inherited from my parents and ancestors.

Finally he told me that unless I had complete bed rest for 2 weeks I would probably never recover, as my body was on the cusp of irreversible deterioration.

Then he consulted my written summary to point out the things I'd missed!

I was amazed and dumbstruck in all, how did he know all this without asking a single question?

But, at last someone knew and understood!

Wow, what an overwhelming sense of relief; my emotions had completely somersaulted.

I was given some phials of "Homeopathic water", and told to take a prescribed number of drops from them at certain times of day, and then return in 2 weeks time.

My progress over the next few months was steady but continuous, though interspersed with plateaus associated with setbacks from another "official rejection" [of] my condition and situation.

During the following year my condition was examined by various Consultants, which included a muscle biopsy at Newcastle University Hospital.

The general diagnostic agreement was that the DNA in the mitochondria in my cells had been damaged by the permethrin insecticide (affecting the Krebs Citric Acid Cycle in the oxidation of glucose), so my energy production and levels were weakened. Though the body had eliminated the chemical the residual damage was permanent with the prognosis: it's incurable, so I would probably need to use a wheelchair for the rest of my life!

In contrast, Dr Melhuish's treatments over the course of the subsequent year, allowed the body to "reprogram" the DNA and restore the normal functioning of the mitochondria and the cells' and body energy production.

So today I live a normal active life without any restrictions; with the exception that I am "chemically naive", so my body is sensitive to food preservations et cetera and chemical sprays and fumes. My body is acting as the "coal miner's canary", warning me of harmful substances in the environment!

But the lasting benefit is the treatment from Dr Melhuish was it has also opened the door for my journey to another aspect of healing outside the conventional paradigms of medical practice. I am now a Shiatsu Therapist, passing on what I have learned to others.

M.S.

A SATISFIED CLIENT

[Message left on my answering machine in May 2014. Verbatim.]

"Hello Dr Melhuish,

This is *[a retired Minister of the Church]*. I saw you 2 weeks ago. Just to let you know that I was picked up in February with a CAT scan with having problems in the bottom of my lungs. I wasn't given any treatment by the Specialist, except you of course. And I was there yesterday, had an x-ray and would you believe the complete gunge that was in my lungs has now disappeared, so I no longer have the problem. And the only treatment I ever received was your treatment. Now isn't that good news. No need to phone me back. Just take the compliment. You are wonderful. Goodbye."

EMPHYSEMA

[Telephone call 1st of November 2014]

"Is that my super Dr in Newburgh? I am just back from 2 weeks holiday in Tenerife. Last November I could only walk 10 to 15 yards; I have been walking up to 2 miles in Tenerife. The other thing is we put a new roof on the garage. I couldn't even have thought of that last year. "

"In percentage terms", I asked, "what would you say the improvement has been?"

"My wife says it's about 80%; I would say it's closer to 50%."

This is a man with Chronic Obstructive Pulmonary Disease (COPD) with emphysema. He is 71 years old.

I gave him 5 treatments Electronic Gem therapy.

[A Dutch colleague of mine received a letter from a retiring Specialist in Respiratory Medicine. The letter stated that in 30 years he had never seen anyone with Emphysema, also called chronic obstructive pulmonary disease (COPD), recover their lung function and congratulated my colleague in having achieved that in a client through using the same treatment method. So there is hope COPD sufferers!].

ANXIETY & DEPRESSION

Dear Roger

... the treatment you gave me and the lifestyle changes you suggested were a turning point in my life and for that I will be forever grateful.

In 2014 I found myself at a point in my life where my depression and anxiety were having a major impact on my life, having affected me for more than a decade. After receiving various different NHS based treatments, including medication, none of which had much success, Dr Melhuish was recommended to me. I was seen very quickly, and diagnosed. Allergies *[Intolerances]* to various food types and hyper sensitivity to certain stimuli were uncovered. Some treatment I received at the point of consultation with follow up natural remedies and life-style changes recommended.

Over the following weeks and months I discovered that my symptoms were diminishing, and gradually disappeared. I was able to function properly for the first time in a long while, I had energy, my mind was able to focus to the point where I could get on with establishing my own business once again. This change is still present today, six years later, as long as I remember to implement those lifestyle changes and continue to avoid the incompatible foods.

The change in my life has been significant and I will be forever thankful to Dr Melhuish for his advice, diagnosis and the caring nature in which I was treated.

RR

AN IMMINENT ACCIDENT

Roger is a wise and compassionate practitioner and a dear friend. I believe that he has literally saved my life on several occasions.

Unlike conventional medical practice, Roger looks at health on different levels, not just the physical symptoms and this gives him and the patient more information. More information means the patient has more choice.

On this occasion when Roger tested me, the significant thing that he told me that was that the way my whole being was configured I was heading towards accident or imminent death. I was given advice and I followed it. Still I was careful, not taking any risks, just in case. But all my caution could not have saved me from what happened soon after.

I was at work and getting ready to go out socially with workmates. At the last moment I was persuaded not to take my car but to get a lift so that could have a glass of wine. We left the building and my friend opened her car, I jumped into the back seat. She reached in and turned on the ignition, the car was in gear, it jumped the kerb and started travelling rapidly down a steep hill. At first, she tried to hold onto the steering wheel, but she had to let go. 'Get out' she screamed at me. I was concerned that if I threw myself out of the car I would get caught up in the wheels, but I had no choice, I had to try as the car was heading for collision with some trees. I threw myself out as far as I could, headfirst, and started rolling down the hill. The car carried on and hit a tree further down. I landed on the road and there was a terrible crack as my head hit the tarmac. My first thought was 'this is serious'. I lay there dazed. There is no doubt in my mind that this was the accident that Roger had talked about and if I had not taken his advice the consequences could have been a lot more serious. I did have a big lump on my head but that was all. I could not stop the accident by being careful and there was no way I could have predicted what was to happen, but I was able to ensure the consequences were less severe.

It is my belief that disease starts in the energy field of your body and if you do not make changes it moves into the physical body. When Roger tested me, some years later, he was able to tell me that energetically I was heading towards pancreatic cancer. Emotionally life had lost its sweetness. Now I knew this I had a choice; did I want to carry on as I had been with the knowledge that this would result in serious illness and early death? Or did I want to make the changes that would allow me to return towards health. Often what is happening to us is on an unconscious level and so we do not have the same choices as I was offered by Roger's testing. Happily, I chose life and health. Once more I was grateful for Roger's intervention. JJ

MYELODYSPLASIA SYNDROME

[NB English is not this lady's first language]

"I would like to say on arriving at Roger home I felt not very optimistic as we had been at many many hospitals and Dr appointments with very little to no satisfaction whatsoever. No matter what medication my husband was given it was useless treatment. When we were at Roger's for the 1st visit he took us into this room with some kind of lights and shone them on my husband for some time, then the next room was like some kind of equipment from the 1930s. I thought oh dear this is the actual Nutty Professor. However after treatment *[my husband]* was amazingly much much better. Roger had almost healed all *[my husband's]* mouth ulcers that good that he could once again talk and eat, he also walked out very spritely as opposed to almost baby steps when we arrived he was so weak. I call Roger our Mr. Roger Einstein and have recommended him to a few friends who have also been very surprised and happy with the outcome. Roger Einstein is an absolute godsend. My husband was given 3 months to live by his Dr. That was 5 years ago. Thank you Roger. IR

LETTERS

Dear Doctor Melhuish, 19/03/95

Just a note to let you know how much your work is appreciated. I came to you roughly 9/10 years ago and felt you gave me the courage to start a change process in my life. Your work is invaluable and you give so much help and inspiration to people that I felt I had to let you know. Please accept my respect and admiration for the help you give to others.

Love,

AH

Dear Roger,

I am compelled to write to you to thank you for all your efforts to bring me back to life. I was a dutiful robot for 60 years but in the past 25 years I have come so alive I am positively looking forward to my next life!

I am truly so very grateful.

Yours alive,

J *[age 85]*

Roger,

Thank you so much for life changing health advice over the past year.

It has literally changed my life.

Kind regards, B

[Previously a type II diabetic with hypertension and irritable bowel, on six different medications. Annual checks confirm he no longer has diabetes, nor hypertension nor irritable bowel. He needs no pharmaceuticals.]

[Another year later]

Hi Roger,

Had my annual diabetes check ... And they continue to be amazed at the results. No sign of diabetes and I have a 4.7 reading. Eyesight and eye scan perfect.

I thank you again for your remarkable treatment which has, literally, changed my life in more ways than one.

B

[Re: Salivary duct stone]

Dear Dr. Melhuish,

[In 1990] I suffered a painful swelling under my jaw affecting tongue and speech but had an appointment at the hospital to have surgery to deal with a blocked salivary gland. Travel to Newburgh with my husband who had an appointment with you. My discomfort was obvious, luckily you spotted this and after hearing my diagnosis you offered to apply acupuncture needles to both earlobes and base of both thumbs plus tincture under tongue. No immediate relief until we arrived home, eruption took place under my tongue – stopper in sink, blood pus and clink – there was a small jaggy calcium stone. Instant relief!

I kept the hospital appointment, Surgeon examined the site and was amazed, no swelling just a small exit wound under the tongue. He was baffled as it was unusual for the stone to eject. No surgery required. No problem thereafter.

Great result for me. Thank you so much.

S

.oOo.

Hi Roger,

[S] here. I used to be a gym member and go every day.

All my life my weight was 14-14.5 stone.

I was told 6 years ago that I had Myelodysplasia syndrome with neutropenia.*[Testing indicated that his bone marrow was toxic with Benzene, from occupational exposure, and Glyphosate, from personal and community use.]*

At my worst *[Dec. 2019]* I went down to 8 stone. The hospital gave me weeks to months to live.

I don't know how my daughter found you but I am so glad she did. It has taken 10 months to gain weight and feel better, but I'm still here.

When I met you I could not speak because of the ulcers *[he had extensive mouth and pharyngeal ulcers. These made it very difficult for speech – he hadn't spoken for 4 months*

– and eating and swallowing were also very painful. It took him a long time and could intake only liquids]. I had no energy at all. 10 months later I am eating, I can speak [he started speaking towards the end of the first treatment], I go a 3 mile walk every day. I am back up to 11 stone. I cannot thank you enough for giving me my life back.

I will thank you until the day I die.

THANK YOU

[S]

[NB After his first visit he also stopped all of his medicines which were: benzydamine, paracetamol, flucloxazole, acyclovir, laxedo, betamethasone, nystatin, doxycycline, morphine slow release patches and oral, given in hospital on a daily basis. This was entirely his choice.

At his third consultation he confided in me that had there been a button on the bed (in hospital) he would have pushed it. He had zero quality of life and wanted to commit suicide. His wife persuaded him to hold on, "there has to be another way" she said.]

FINAL COMMENT

Thank you for investing your curiosity and time to read this book.

This is how far I have come beyond convention, seeing the Human Being as an energy system in which disruption to that flow creates illness.

Your route into illness is unique to you. The processes I have learned see and honour that individuality.

All illnesses acquired in life have the potential to be reversed or, put another way, if the body has produced the illness it has to be possible to *un*-produce that illness.

All such illnesses have an aspect of food intolerance. We have not evolved to eat the refined sugars, the milk products, the coffees, colas, tea, chocolate; our illnesses are evidence of that.

My dearest hope is that you can grasp the power that is within you and make some changes which can literally change your life in a similar way to those who have kindly written to me over the years, some of which is expressed 'In their own write'.

Enjoy your journey along this magical ride that is life.

May you maximise your health, fill yourself with laughter at every opportunity, be at peace and go with Love.

Roger Melhuish

ABOUT THE AUTHOR

Roger Melhuish spent the first five years of his life in Africa before returning to Bristol in South-West England. Scotland was to become his adopted home from 1965 when he fell in love with it on his first trip to St Andrews.

Roger completed his medical training in the conventional way, spending several years working through gruelling hospital shifts, before becoming a GP.

His foray into complementary health began with a course in osteopathy. Impressed by the results it enabled and fascinated at the magnitude of what else there was to learn, Roger continued to expand his extra-curricular study. After training in medical acupuncture and homeopathy, his thirst for novel approaches continued. Ultimately this led to an eclectic and highly unconventional practice that he still uses today, and which earned him the 'Witch Doctor' eponym from a grateful World Champion.

In addition to the impressive array of knowledge and skills that Roger has amassed, his intuitive abilities are outstanding. He has a way of looking at things that is always different and an inexplicable ability to see things that are invisible to others.

Now in his mid-70s, Roger works with even deeper wisdom and compassion. He still feels immense joy in doing what he does and is often moved to tears by the expressions of gratitude from his clients.

He always replies "Thank you. It is a privilege."

SUGGESTED READING

- *The Music of Life* by Hazrat Inyat Khan
- *Talking Sense* by Richard Asher, published c 1970
- *The Body Keeps the Score* by Bessel van der Kolk
- *Not All In the Mind* by Richard Mackarness
- *Electromagnetic Man* by Cyril Smith and Simon Best, published by JM Dent and Sons Ltd, London
- *The Biology of Belief* by Bruce Lipton, Ph.D published by Hay House, London
- *The Tibetan Book of Living and Dying* by Sogyal Rinpoche, published by Rider
- *A Plague of Corruption* by Judy Mikovits Ph.D and Kent Heckenlively by Skyhorse Publishing
- *The Truth About the Drug Companies* by Marcia Angell, MD by Random House, New York
- *Lifespan* by David Sinclair PhD, published by Atria Books, Simon and Schuster; UK edition by Thorsons
- *The Microwave Delusion* by Brian Stein and Jonathan Mantle published by Grosvenor House Publishing, Link House, Tolworth, KT6 7 HT, UK.
- *Dissolving Illusions* by Suzanne Humphries MD and Roman Bystrianyk, printed by Amazon
- *Anyone Who Tells You Vaccination is Safe and Effective is Lying* by Dr Vernon Coleman, printed by Amazon
- *The Iodine Crisis* by Lynne Farrow published by Devon Press NY
- *The Truth about Vaccines* by Ty Bollinger

Zulu saying:

Umuntu ongazi

Ucabanga ukuthi uyazi,

Kanti akazi lutho

Owaziyo uvele

The person who doesn't know thinks he knows,

and yet he knows nothing at all.

The one who knows

Just does it,

And sure enough

It happens.

Printed in Great Britain
by Amazon